KU-346-957

The City Cats

Sammy was looking for a way across the busy road. There were lulls in the traffic flow and he thought he and Pinkie should be able to make use of one of these.

'We'll have to dart over like a pair of hares,' he advised Pinkie.

'It's too dangerous,' Pinkie warned. 'We'll be flattened!'

'Nonsense,' said Sammy. 'The humans are crossing over all the time. You have to wait until the noise has died down, then race for it. Besides, we can't stay here for ever.'

Pinkie saw there was no alternative. There came a lull in the traffic and she saw Sammy tense his muscles.

By the same author:

The Ram of Sweetriver
The King of the Vagabonds
The Beach Dogs
Just Nuffin
A Great Escape
A Legacy of Ghosts
Colin Dann Animal Stories (3-in-1 collection)

The Farthing Wood Series:

Animals of Farthing Wood
In the Grip of Winter
Fox's Feud
Fox Cub Bold
The Siege of White Deer Park
In the Path of the Storm
Battle For The Park

The
City Cats
COLIN DANN

RED FOX

A Red Fox Book
Published by Random House Children's Books
20 Vauxhall Bridge Road, London SW1V 2SA

A division of Random House UK Ltd

London Melbourne Sydney Auckland
Johannesburg and agencies throughout the world

First published in Great Britain in 1991 by
Hutchinson Children's Books

Red Fox edition 1992
Reprinted 1993

Copyright © Colin Dann 1991

The right of Colin Dann to be identified as the author
of this work has been asserted by them in accordance
with the Copyright, Designs and Patents Act, 1988

This book is sold subject to the condition that it shall
not, by way of trade or otherwise, be lent, resold, hired
out, or otherwise circulated without the publisher's
prior consent in any form of binding or cover other
than that in which it is published and without a similar
condition including this condition being imposed on
the subsequent purchaser

Printed and bound in Great Britain by
Cox & Wyman Ltd, Reading, Berkshire

ISBN 0 09 993890 1

For Anneka

Contents

1 Removed 1
2 Released 7
3 The park 16
4 The flat 25
5 Escape 35
6 Toby 44
7 Along the canal 53
8 Miles apart 61
9 Cat and mouse 71
10 Trust and mistrust 78
11 The heart of London 87
12 Toby turns 96
13 Go north! 104
14 Mother love 111
15 You're going to see your father 122
16 The fate of four cats 130

—1—

Removed

Sammy and Pinkie were alone in Quartermile Field. After Sammy had established himself as King of the Vagabonds all the other cats had dispersed, one by one. They hadn't cared to remain in the neighbourhood under the supremacy of the young tabby. Once it was certain his days as leader were over, Sammy's father, Brute, had shown the way by leaving. Only the lame black cat, Scruff, stayed, hidden away in the rank undergrowth. He posed no threat and was in any case not fit enough to move far off.

Pinkie, the little white cat with the pink ears and nose that had given her her name, was Sammy's chosen mate. She rubbed herself against his coat, arching her back and nuzzling him in the darkness. She knew Sammy wouldn't desert her and had, at last, put his domestic upbringing behind him. 'We have the whole area to ourselves,' she purred. 'There's no competition, no rivalry remaining. We have the pick of everything.'

Sammy was aware he had won this position for them. His strength and endurance had been tried and tested and he had emerged victorious. He was lean and tough, a cunning and clever hunter. 'Yes, we shall do well here,' he answered Pinkie. 'It's a good place to make our own.'

Quartermile Field was indeed a good place for feral cats. Pinkie had grown up there, born into the way of life

that Sammy had chosen to adopt. The place had plenty of
shelter. There was good hunting. Rabbits frequently
strayed on to the site, as well as the mice and voles and
birds that normally inhabited it. And it was sufficiently
close to human dwellings that when times got hard, scraps
and waste from their kitchens made a useful substitute for
live prey. The pair of cats had everything they needed.

With no challengers to his role as the dominant cat of the
area Sammy found his new way of life very satisfying. He
went where he chose and everywhere he went Pinkie
accompanied him. There was no scarcity of prey and the
necessary wiles he had acquired for catching it made his
task only as difficult as he permitted it to be. He and
Pinkie shared all their catches and as the weeks wore on
the two cats began to put on weight.

The only threat now to the cats' well-being was the
weather. Sammy had never forgotten his father's description of the conditions in winter-time. As the days
shortened and grew colder Sammy ranged farther afield,
his wanderings bounded only by the impassable torrent of
a vast river. He wanted to become familiar with a wider
area than that of his immediate surroundings – to seek out
any potential food resource that might prove of use in less
easy circumstances. He went beyond Quartermile Field
and the houses and gardens nearby, beyond the woods
and meadows he had already explored. Roaming was in
his blood – Brute, a great roamer, was responsible for that.

But when the weather grew cold, every creature's
movements were curtailed, Sammy's along with them.
Only the need to provide themselves with food made
animals stir from their warm burrows or tunnels. And
then Sammy was waiting for them, patiently and
confidently.

But as the cold bit deeper, the rabbits stopped coming

to the old allotment plots on the other side of the high wire fence which skirted Quartermile Field. Ice and snow kept them closer to their warren. Then the smaller prey – mice, voles or shrews – diminished in number. More vulnerable to the harshness of the prevailing temperatures, many of them succumbed. Only the stoutest survived and these, by their very natures, were more successful at evading predators. So Sammy, Pinkie, and Scruff too, began to feel the prick of hunger. Brute's words seemed to ring in Sammy's ears each time he hunted and returned without a catch to his and Pinkie's shelter in the broken shed. Winter. Scarcity. Hunger. These were the three strands which held them fast and from which it seemed they couldn't break free.

As the winter made its relentless presence felt Sammy turned his attention, as he had once before, to human habitations. There was always food of a sort to be had around houses. Pinkie accompanied him on his forays into gardens. Sammy never ceased to marvel at the unerring way in which she rooted out every valuable titbit. He was a supreme hunter but Pinkie was his superior in providing food in their straitened circumstances.

'You're a wonder,' he said admiringly as they crouched one evening in the snow against the lee side of a garden shed. He had been convinced there had been no chance of their stomachs being filled. Two or three centimetres of snow had fallen, covering everything on the ground. Yet Pinkie had uncovered some nourishing strips of fat thrown out for birds before the snowfall.

'I could smell them,' she answered simply. 'I've been doing this sort of thing all my life.' But when they had devoured the cold hard scraps she began to purr, nestling against Sammy. She was pleased.

Sammy recalled another vagabond. 'I wonder how

Scruff will manage?' he murmured. They had caught no glimpse of him for days.

'Nobody better than he at unearthing every last scrap,' said Pinkie. 'I once saw him eating worms. He's a survivor.' She wasn't greatly concerned with Scruff's problems. In the world into which she had been born it was every cat for itself.

By morning the ground was frozen hard. Only the main road that ran past the wilderness that was Quartermile Field was comparatively clear, the motor traffic having prevented the snow from settling on it overmuch. In the early hours, however, the road was quiet. Sammy and Pinkie paced along it. Sammy wanted to know where it led. His curiosity drove him now to explore as far as he could in the direction away from the river. His tabby coat was duller than usual whilst Pinkie's stood out clearly, whiter than the trampled snow. Set well back from the road was the cottage of Mrs Lambert, Sammy's old mistress. He passed by without turning his head. His eyes were fixed on a distant point where men were moving around a large vehicle. It was barely light.

Sammy was interested in the human activity. Because he had been brought up in their care he was aware of the kindliness of people. He was only half wild. But Pinkie had never known Sammy's early kind of existence. She didn't trust humans and had never formed an attachment to any. She had only accepted food from an old woman who had interested herself in the welfare of the vagabond cats. She had come no closer to human contact than that and she didn't wish to do so. As she and Sammy neared the parked vehicle she hung back. The men were unloading furniture from a removal van and the noise they were creating was almost enough to send her scurrying. She hesitated, flinching at each sound.

Sammy continued, unmindful of Pinkie's wariness. Presently he sat down in the gutter to watch more closely. A strong odour of cooked food emanated from the van. Over many months countless hamburgers and fish and chip suppers, consumed hastily in the cab during the men's snatched moments of rest, had pervaded the fabric of the vehicle. Sammy licked his chops and waited. He thought an opportunity might arise for further investigation. The men paid him little heed. There was no time to waste on a stray cat when hefty furniture had to be shifted.

Sammy was patient. The smell from the lorry was so inviting it was impossible to ignore. The men carried on humping and heaving. The vehicle emptied. Sammy looked round, expecting to find Pinkie had returned home. He understood her suspicion of human contraptions, but she hadn't bolted. She squatted perhaps fifty metres away, still and silent, her eyes on her mate.

Finally the men had done. They left the ramp of the vehicle down and went into the house for well-earned mugs of tea. The van's interior loomed dark and empty save for a few boxes and chests. Sammy waited a few moments longer. The savoury smell stole through the crisp air and assailed his nostrils afresh. He ventured a step or two forwards, sniffing eagerly. He reached the ramp. He looked round. There was no sign of the men returning. In a trice he was up and into the van, searching systematically in every corner for the source of that delicious smell. Minutes later Pinkie edged forward too. She had caught an unmistakable whiff of fried fish. Some of the old wrappings of the men's takeaway meals still littered the floor of the cab. She miaowed to Sammy. 'Is it safe?'

Sammy paused from his search. 'Perfectly safe,' he assured her. 'There's something in here for us if we're quick.'

Pinkie followed him into the van. The quietness of its hollow interior encouraged her.

'It's just *finding* it that's difficult,' Sammy complained. 'You're more expert than I am, Pinkie. You'll probably go straight to it.'

They were far down the length of the lorry, hidden behind some boxes when the removal men came back. One of the men hurled a pair of tea-chests inside, then hitched the ramp back into the interior. He shut the doors with a slam that echoed horribly inside the lorry, terrifying the trapped cats. Then the entire vehicle throbbed as the engine was started. The men, their work done, began to sing as the van pulled away from the kerb for the return journey. The two cats cowered in the back, all thought of food forgotten as they listened to the din of the men's voices. They had no idea what was happening to them – that with every jolt and rumble of the wheels beneath, they were being carried farther away from the place that they called their home.

—2—

Released

The van had evidently come a long way to deliver its load, for the cats' misery seemed to have no end. Yet after hours of suffering the motion of the vehicle they gradually became used to it. The noise, though, was different. They couldn't get used to that. It was appalling; the engine, the roar of other traffic, the piercing shrillness of the cab radio and the men's booming voices. Their only consolation was that the heat from the lorry's engine kept them warm. At last they thought their ordeal had come to an end. The lorry stopped. The men left the cab, their voices receding as they walked away. Sammy and Pinkie, crouching amongst the debris on the metal floor, stayed motionless, thoroughly numbed by their horrible experience. Slowly, the welcome quietness restored their spirits.

'They've gone, I'm sure of it,' Sammy said in a low voice.

'Do you think so? Oh, if only you're right!' Pinkie wailed. She had never been so shaken up.

Still, they waited, hardly daring to stir in the darkness. Finally Sammy plucked up courage. He stretched and began to search in earnest for a way out. A chink of light here and there was his only guide. His enormously dilated pupils roved around the long container. Wherever he moved, his whiskers encountered obstacles, brushing boxes and chests and the imprisoning metal walls. He realized now that the absence of the men was of no advantage to them. He and Pinkie couldn't escape from their prison without human help.

Pinkie had come to the same conclusion. 'Sammy, you're to blame for this,' she accused him. 'Why did you have to bother with humans and their things which we don't understand? I've never trusted them. Oh, why did we have to climb into here? Now we're trapped!'

Sammy was astonished at the new tone in Pinkie's voice, one he had never heard before. But she was simply very frightened. He tried to calm her down. 'Don't worry,' he said. 'We'll get out the same way we got in. We must be patient. The men will let us out.'

'The men have gone!' she hissed.

'Yes, I know. But this monster belongs to them, so they must come back.'

'When?'

'Well – some time.' Sammy's optimism was draining away.

Pinkie fell silent. Sammy lay down again. It was futile to continue searching. The cats listened to the drone and rush of passing traffic. Then their ears pricked up. Men's voices were again approaching the vehicle. The cab doors were opened, then slammed shut. The engine burst once more into life, the jangle of the radio began anew. Sammy and Pinkie's journey was not yet over. The men had only made a brief lunch stop. Now the cats' ordeal continued as the second leg of the journey back to base began.

There were no fresh alarms for the unwilling travellers; just the same jolting, buffeting racket as before. The two cats lay side by side, finding a sort of solace in their closeness. Pinkie said, 'I'm sorry I blamed you, Sammy. You weren't to know; the smell of food was very tempting. And yet, there is no food, is there?'

'No,' said Sammy glumly. 'Not until we are released from here.'

Eventually the removal van reached its destination. It was driven into the company yard and parked. The men's day was over.

The winter dusk descended. The lorry grew colder and colder. Later the yard gates were closed. Sammy and Pinkie had a long night ahead of them. They miaowed in protest, then in desperation. But there was no one around to hear and they soon tired themselves out. They were very hungry and thirsty and they thought about Quarter-mile Field, the rigours of which seemed so mild by comparison with their present predicament.

'It's so cold,' Pinkie complained. She paced up and down, unable to rest. 'Oh, I wish I were Scruff at this moment!'

'You can't mean that,' Sammy remarked. 'Scruff's lame and old. But if you're thinking you wish you were where Scruff *is* at this moment, I agree with you.'

'We'll never see Quartermile Field again, I know it,' Pinkie said. 'It seems far distant now; it's so long since we ventured into this horrible great box.'

Sammy longed to be able to do something. He hated being shut up like this at the mercy of human beings, however kindly they might be. The thing he prized above everything else, his independence, was lost.

During the night the cats continued to cry out every time they heard a sound in case someone helpful was nearby. Their miaowing from the depths of the container was inaudible although they didn't know it. They did catnap from time to time. There was nothing else for them to do. But even the longest night must come to an end. So when the late-arriving winter daylight finally peeped through the chinks in the lorry's frame their hopes rose.

'Let's get down to the end where we jumped in,' Sammy

suggested. 'Then as soon as the men open this up we'll dash out before they really know we've been here.'

'Where do we dash to?' Pinkie questioned.

'To – to – the safest place!' Sammy answered hesitatingly.

'Where's that? We don't know where we are.'

'Just follow me,' Sammy said. 'Wherever I go, you keep up with me. But first, be ready to jump clear!'

They squatted by the tail of the removal van and waited. For a long time nothing happened. 'It feels as if we've been here for ever,' Pinkie moaned. Then they did hear evidence of life in the neighbourhood – motor traffic, footsteps, voices, bangs and thumps; all the sounds of another day of human activity beginning. It was a while before any of these sounds came close to where they were trapped. Then there was a rattle and a whine as the yard gates were unlocked and opened. Footsteps, voices approached the van. The cats tensed. A louder rattle. The doors behind which they crouched were about to be flung wide.

The cats didn't wait longer than necessary. As soon as there was a crack of daylight between the doors wide enough to emit a cat's body, Sammy burst forth, then Pinkie, startling the man standing at the back of the lorry so much that he actually jumped. 'Blimey – what's this?' he exclaimed.

Sammy instinctively fled towards the open yard gates, with Pinkie in hot pursuit. They raced through and on to the pavement outside. They found themselves in a lane with tall buildings on either side which offered no shelter or hiding-place. They kept running. They felt as though they were in a sort of tunnel, but ahead they could see where the lane opened out into a wider street. Now Sammy slowed his pace to a walk and Pinkie did likewise. They needed to be careful; to use their natural feline caution. They didn't know what lay before them; moreover, the lane was empty so there was no danger for them there. Every so often, at the lane's junction with the street, they saw motor vehicles pass by. It was still early morning and the traffic was light. They understood about traffic. It was a common sight in their home area and they knew it was something to avoid at all costs.

'There's no snow here,' Pinkie remarked with surprise.

'All the better for us,' said Sammy, 'when we come to hunt.'

They were reminded of their hunger. Their priorities now were to satisfy that and find somewhere safe to shelter. Sammy paused to take a few laps from the edge of a puddle where ice hadn't formed. He and Pinkie had warmed themselves up by their headlong dash. Sammy's confidence was returning now that the cats' freedom was restored to them. They ambled on to the end of the lane, keeping close to the wall on their left. Pinkie made sure she kept close behind Sammy as he crept to the opening.

What he saw made him recoil involuntarily. It was all so strange: enormous buildings which dwarfed anything he had ever seen before. Rows of parked cars and other vehicles; pavements dotted with metal and concrete posts and signs of all sizes and descriptions; a wide street which, despite the early hour, already had more movement in it than he had ever witnessed in his home area; people walking quickly and purposefully by; huge moving vehicles, bigger even than the removal lorry, with two tiers of people inside.

'What is it?' mewed Pinkie.

'I – don't know,' Sammy muttered. 'It's – it's – wonderful.'

And he didn't know – and of course neither did Pinkie – that they had been carried from their old haunts and deposited in the heart of a great city. Sammy was fascinated by all that was new to him. Strangely enough, he wasn't frightened. Keeping perfectly still, he stared at this panorama of a London thoroughfare which, with each minute, seemed to expand as its tempo quickened relentlessly.

Pinkie inched forward to his side. 'We – we can't –' she began but she didn't finish. She was struck dumb. The gathering mass of movement of a London working day was breathtaking. She caught sight of a pair of sparrows chirruping on a low gutter. 'We need to find food,' she reminded Sammy.

Sammy lost his look of absorption. 'Yes,' he said. 'And there should be plenty of titbits for two hungry cats amongst all these people.'

'Are you going to *beg* food?'

'No, we're going to nose it out. You're so expert, you're bound to find something. But this time, Pinkie, we'll stay out in the open. No more straying inside human enclosures. Come on!' Sammy slipped round the wall and into the street. He walked boldly along the pavement, past a row of shops. The smell of food was unmistakable. But he wasn't going to venture inside those buildings. Oh no! He was searching for those scraps that careless humans often left behind.

Pinkie was far more nervous of her surroundings. The blare of the city was frightening and the bigness of everything made her feel of no consequence. She didn't realize that this was a positive advantage to herself and Sammy. For most of the hurrying pedestrians were far too preoccupied to notice two stray cats. One or two turned their heads to look at Pinkie who was small and pretty. Sammy, with his dark tabby coat, lean appearance and crossed-out face didn't attract any glances.

The tabby found a discarded burger carton outside a takeaway restaurant. There were some pieces of meat still inside. He and Pinkie stopped briefly to eat, taking the food at a gulp. They wanted more. Sammy sniffed around. Some cold chips, covered in sauce, were all he could find. This was a new food, but it was all grist to the mill of the cats' hunger. They were quite used to accepting almost anything edible in their diet, even in Quartermile Field. Sammy, however, meant to explore the hunting possibilities of the area as soon as he could. Human food served its purpose but it could never be as good as freshly caught prey.

The pavement was becoming increasingly congested with people and the cats slunk close to the shop fronts to avoid being trodden on. Across the street there was a gap visible in the buildings where they could see a patch of green – an oasis they had to reach. They both now wanted to get out of the mêlée. But how to cross that fearsome street?

The parked vehicles on their side of the road offered the cats some protection. Sammy led the way. They threaded their way through the striding legs of the passers-by and dived under a car. It was quieter and secluded there but they flinched each time the traffic roared past. As long as they didn't run out, they were quite safe. However, Sammy was looking for a way across the busy road. There were lulls in the traffic flow and he thought he and Pinkie should be able to make use of one of these.

'We'll have to dart over like a pair of hares,' he advised Pinkie.

'It's too dangerous,' Pinkie warned. 'We'll be flattened!'

'Nonsense,' said Sammy. 'The humans are crossing over all the time. You have to wait until the noise has died down, then race for it. Besides, we can't stay here for ever.'

Pinkie saw there was no alternative. There came a lull in the traffic and she saw Sammy tense his muscles.

'Now!' he hissed. They streaked out from the parked car, their eyes set on the green patch on the opposite side of the road. They didn't stop running until they were across the other pavement and in through the park entrance. Pinkie was delighted with the calm that now encompassed them. They had left the rush and row of the street and found themselves in a wide expanse of green grass and trees as far as their eyes could see. At that hour the park was almost empty of people.

'This looks like the sort of place we're used to,' said Pinkie. 'Let's explore.'

'Take care,' Sammy cautioned, 'there may be other cats about.'

They avoided the footpaths and trotted together over the short winter grass. They saw no cats but they did see some squirrels and, more especially, pigeons. Flocks of pigeons could be found wherever there was a suggestion of human leftovers: around litter bins or park benches where crusts and crumbs had been dropped. Sammy and Pinkie were quick to spot a likely source of food and the sight of the pigeons led them on to a tour of the nearest litter bins. Most of these had recently been emptied. Pinkie didn't hesitate to jump on top of each one where she balanced precariously on the rim while sniffing out the contents. She saw only paper and plastic. The pigeons, of course, scattered at the cats' approach, flapping nervously up to the nearest branches. Sammy was far more interested in the possibilities they offered his hunting prowess than in the contents of the bins.

'There's a regular source of food there,' he commented as the birds wheeled about, alternately settling and rising again. 'No problem to catch. They're clumsy on the ground and a bit slow in their take-off.' He was eager to test his abilities again.

'Go on then, great hunter,' drawled Pinkie, 'catch us something to eat.'

Sammy looked around, waiting for the birds to risk dropping to the ground again. He knew that if he and Pinkie kept quite still, the birds would think all was safe. Sure enough, the pigeons began, in twos and threes, to come down from the leafless boughs. Hunger was the prime driving force for them too. Sammy's eyes narrowed as he watched each bird carefully. He soon picked out one that moved awkwardly over the grass. It appeared to have a damaged foot and tended to hobble. Keeping close to the ground he crept forward, stalking this bird expertly. He froze when the bird faced him, then moved again when it turned the other way. He had the instinctive technique of a lion hunting antelope in the African bush. The pigeon had very little chance. Sammy made a final rush when he guessed he was close enough and pounced on the bird at the very instant it realized it had left flight too late. The other pigeons were airborne as Sammy's claws and teeth fastened on to his prey. He picked the pigeon up in his jaws and carried it proudly back to Pinkie.

'Well done,' said the little white cat. 'You've made a good beginning for us. This is our first real meal in these strange parts. And we'll need all the strength we can muster to get ourselves back to Quartermile Field.'

—3—

The park

Sammy had no intention of going back to Quartermile Field, even if he had known how to set about it. He was excited by the speed of city life. Everything moved at a different pace, particularly the humans. They had none of the ambling dreaminess of people in the country. He thought of his old mistress, Mrs Lambert, and tried to picture her amongst the hurrying throngs on the city pavements. And then he began to wonder what the local population of cats would be like – born and bred amidst the buzz of the metropolis. He thought he would soon find out.

He and Pinkie had found a sheltered area in the park to eat their catch. There were fenced enclosures and the two cats had slipped through the railings and crouched amongst the thick evergreen shrubs, confident they would he undisturbed. While they ate, Sammy mused.

'You know, Pinkie,' he said, looking around at the thick cover provided by the profusion of plants, 'we could make this our base. There's plenty of cover and we'd be well screened when we sleep.'

'Yes,' said Pinkie, 'I suppose we should be cautious and stay put for the rest of the winter.'

'Of course we must. And, we'll soon get used to our new life.'

Pinkie looked at her mate. Did she detect satisfaction, even excitement, in Sammy's voice? She couldn't be certain.

A spell of very cold but dry weather prevailed for the next week. Sammy and Pinkie kept on the move during the dark hours. Most of the day they huddled together in the midst of a stand of ornamental bamboo which kept the frost at bay. There were thick dry leaves to nestle in and the two cats wrapped their tails around their noses as they slept. They saw few humans except for an occasional hearty walker taking exercise in the crisp invigorating air. The cats found a great lake which was frozen from shore to shore. Waterfowl of all sizes skittered across the ice, puzzled by the disappearance of the water. Inshore many more skulked in the vegetation, uttering their strident calls to one another. The birds were ravenous and flocked to each scrap of bread thrown by sympathetic humans. The competition for food was so fierce that fights were constantly breaking out. Pigeons and seagulls and sparrows strove for their share of the spoils amongst the ducks and geese, coots and moorhens. It was at these times that Sammy and Pinkie were most likely to catch the birds off guard. Sammy was becoming adept at hunting large birds and one day he caught a duck. He and Pinkie dragged it off into the bushes almost before it knew what had happened to it.

The duck was sufficient food for them for two days. As long as the lake remained frozen the waterfowl became Sammy's favourite targets. 'We'll never starve here,' he said. 'I don't understand why others don't make use of this glut of meat.'

'Others?' Pinkie queried. 'What others?' She sat looking at her mate with a self-satisfied cat-smile on her face. Sammy was the greatest hunter she had known. Even

Brute, his father, had never caught prey like this. She licked her chops as she waited for Sammy's answer.

'I'm talking about other cats,' he said. 'Where are they all? We can't be the only ones around here.'

'Oh, of course there are *pets*,' Pinkie said contemptuously. 'With so many human dwellings in the area there are bound to be plenty of them. But they wouldn't come here, would they?'

'Why not? We all like to explore, whether we're pets or – or –'

'Or like us,' Pinkie said sweetly, 'predators.'

Predators. Sammy liked that word. Yes, he and Pinkie were predators and, as far as they could tell, the only ones in this city park. They had seen dogs but, big and fierce-looking as these sometimes were, they were not predators. Their movements were restricted, they were at the beck and call of their owners. Sammy decided that he must be the fiercest animal in the whole area. It made him feel stronger and more fearless than ever. Birds panicked at his approach – except the swans who were too massive for him to kill. But all the others around the lake and through the park were wary of him.

Despite all this Sammy was dissatisfied. What was the good of being the terror of the park, of having such a reputation if only Pinkie, squirrels and jittery birds knew about it. He wanted others to know. And that meant other cats.

In between his hunting activities Sammy spent more and more time searching for signs of other cats. He didn't care if they were pets, he wanted them to know about him. Pinkie let him wander on his own. She was expecting the birth of their kittens and was beginning to feel less active.

One day Sammy was late returning to their lair. Dawn had broken and Pinkie busied herself with collecting as much comfortable bedding as she could find for the imminent event. Sammy had wandered to one end of the park as far as the canal. The sluggish water fascinated him and reminded him of that great river he had seen at home, although the canal, of course, had none of its power. While he was contemplating whether the two stretches of water might have a connection he heard a series of strange noises – animal noises. By the sound of them they couldn't have been all that far distant. He heard whoops and howls, roars and shrieks, sounds such as he had never before experienced. What were these strange animals? Did they live in the park? And was this the reason he had seen no other cats? They sounded powerful beasts, these that gave voice as day was heralded. Sammy was alarmed and ran. He wasn't quite ready for an encounter even though he had begun to believe himself all-powerful.

As he ran, his mind was fully occupied with thoughts of great beasts, bigger than dogs, roaming the park while all the time he and Pinkie had been confident they had it to themselves. How foolish they had been and how fortunate not to have crossed their path. He must get back and warn Pinkie. Forgetting to look, he darted out across a track. The next thing he knew his left foreleg was caught up and wrenched agonisingly in a sort of whirling trap. Sammy screeched a long miaow of pain. He had blundered into a bicycle and his leg was tangled in the spokes of its wheel.

The cyclist braked sharply and jumped off. Sammy struggled to free himself. The man found it difficult to quieten the cat sufficiently to tend him. Eventually Sammy wrenched his leg free and limped away. He had been badly frightened by the metal machine that had caused him so much pain and wanted nothing of the rueful cyclist's attempts to soothe him.

Sammy's leg was not broken but the muscles and ligaments in his shoulder were badly torn. He couldn't put any weight on his leg and the pain was excruciating.

Howling in misery he finally collapsed on the frosty
ground under a park bench. The cyclist watched him for a
moment, then pedalled on, persuading himself that the
cat would survive.

Sammy rested awhile. The damaged leg caused him
agony. Day broadened. A brilliant winter's day was
beginning. The frost melted. The sun was warm as it
shone over the park. Sammy pulled himself into the
sunlight, blinked in the fierce sparkling rays and again lay
down. He thought of Pinkie. Now, in full daylight, there
seemed no threat from wild animals. His head drooped.
He fell asleep.

Hours later, he awoke to a new surge of pain and to the
sound of a gentle voice. A young woman who worked in a
nearby office, had been taking a lunch-time stroll in the
park. Luckily for Sammy, this young woman was very
fond of cats, though she didn't have one of her own. She
had seen Sammy and Pinkie on other occasions and knew
that they were semi-wild. At first, when she had stopped
to look at the sleeping cat she hadn't realized there was
anything wrong with him. Tentatively, she had stretched
out a hand to stroke him. Sammy woke as her hand
touched his shoulder.

'Oh dear, poor thing,' said the girl as Sammy winced.
'What's wrong with you, are you hurt?'

Sammy blinked at her. He had not entirely forgotten his
domestic upbringing and he could still respond to words
of kindness.

'Let's have a look at you,' the girl whispered. She
touched him here and there very gently and soon discovered where the problem lay. 'You've been injured,
haven't you? Poor creature, poor creature. . . .' She
squatted by the tabby cat pondering her best course of
action. She knew he needed attention but she wasn't
equipped just then to give him any help. She needed a bag

or a basket to put him in. She meant to get him to a vet. She consulted her watch. If she was quick, she decided, she could get back to her office and fetch something suitable to carry him in, then return, before she was due to begin work again. But would the animal stay where he was? Well, she'd have to risk that. She reflected that he probably wasn't capable of moving very far in his present state. She stood up slowly so as not to frighten Sammy and set off, walking very briskly, and sometimes breaking into a trot.

At her office she found a colleague had a capacious shoulder bag which would suit her purpose perfectly. She begged the woman to lend it to her.

'Oh, Lizzie, why go to all this bother for a stray?' the woman remarked. 'It'll be just like a wild thing. It won't let you come near it.'

'It's already done that, Penny,' said the girl. 'I'm sure it knows I want to help. Do let me try. You can put your things in *my* bag for the moment.'

'Oh well – I suppose I can't refuse.' Penny smiled. 'But then what? You can't bring the cat back here!'

'It's just for the afternoon,' said Lizzie. 'It'll sleep if it's not well.'

'You'd better keep it out of the boss's sight then.'

'Oh, Mr Searle's as big a softie as I am when it comes to animals,' Lizzie laughed. '*He* won't object.'

When the shoulder bag had been emptied she hurried back to the park. Sammy hadn't moved. When he saw Lizzie approaching he miaowed a greeting.

'I knew you'd be pleased to see me,' she said affectionately. 'Now then, I hope you're going to let me lift you because I want to look after you.' She bent down and gently, very gently, eased her hands under Sammy's body. Sammy made no objection apart from a muffled squeal of pain. He understood the young woman had come to help.

What he didn't know, however, was that she planned to take him away from the park. He allowed himself to be raised and deposited in the shoulder bag.

'That's it,' said Lizzie brightly, zipping up the bag so that there was just enough room for Sammy to put his head out. 'We'll soon have you more comfortable.' And she set off once more for her office.

The pain of his accident had driven all thought of strange fierce-sounding animals from Sammy's head, but he hadn't forgotten Pinkie and he soon realized that the young woman was not carrying him back to his mate but farther away from her. From the opening in the bag he watched the park receding into the distance and he began to protest. Lizzie, of course, ignored his miaows. 'It's all right,' she told him as she strode along the street, 'we're nearly there. Then you can rest for the afternoon.'

The last thing Sammy wanted to do was rest. He tried to struggle out of the bag but he was zipped up tight and, in any case, as soon as he attempted to move the pain in his shoulder made him desist. So he was restricted to more and more desperate cries of anguish at this forced separation from Pinkie. Lizzie soon reached her office and placed Sammy in a corner near her desk where she could keep an eye on him.

Penny regarded the cat with considerable misgiving. 'That's a new bag,' she said. 'I hope he doesn't mess it up.'

'You can hold me responsible,' said Lizzie with a wave of her hand. 'I'll replace it if necessary.'

Penny thought she had taken offence. 'No need to go to those lengths,' she assured her. 'But – I suppose you're going to take him home?'

'Yes. And how did you know he's a *he?*'

'I didn't. He just looks like a *he*,' said Penny. 'He's not very beautiful, is he, with that stripe running right across his face?'

'Does it matter?'

'Well, no, not really. Er – look, Lizzie, I *shall* need my bag back before we go home.'

'Of course. Don't worry, I'll go down to the post room and get a carton later.'

The warmth of the office was such a contrast to the bitter cold of the park that Sammy soon felt drowsy. When Mr Searle came past Lizzie's desk on his return from lunch he saw the bag with Sammy's head sticking out of one end with his eyes blissfully closed. 'Hallo – what's this? Pet's Corner?' he joked.

Lizzie explained the circumstances and begged him to be tolerant about the cat for just this one afternoon.

'Oh – nonsense,' her boss brushed it aside. 'I think you're to be congratulated, showing such concern for the poor animal. Are you anywhere near a vet?'

Lizzie nodded. 'There's an evening surgery so I can take him tonight.'

Sammy dozed for most of the afternoon. Occasionally he uttered a plaintive miaow. Lizzie fetched a cardboard carton from the post room which she lined thickly with tissues. Then, before transferring Sammy to the box, she poured some milk into a saucer and placed it under her desk. Then she unzipped Penny's bag and lifted him out. Sammy hadn't seen or tasted milk since his early days as a kitten in Mrs Lambert's care. He sniffed at the saucer and immediately recalled the flavour. He drank thirstily while Penny surreptitiously examined her shoulder bag. She was pleased to see it hadn't suffered too much.

There were no more protests from Sammy. He was too tired and too miserable to show any fight. Lizzie put him in the box, sellotaped it closed save for an air-hole and took it down, Sammy inside, to the post room where one of the packers made a handle for it out of some sisal string. Sammy was ready for his visit to the vet's.

—4—

The flat

Lizzie Reed took the tube from Regent's Park to Warwick Avenue. Only a short walk away from there she had a basement flat in a large house near the canal. She didn't stop to eat but went straight to the vet's. Sammy was given a sedative and examined thoroughly. He needed lots of rest, the vet said, to enable his bruised ligaments and muscles to heal. He suggested Lizzie keep him caged.

'How would I do that?' she asked.

'Well, a tea-chest is ideal, providing he has air, light and . . .'

'Oh, I don't have anything like that,' Lizzie interrupted disappointedly. 'He's a stray that I picked up and I want to look after him.'

'So he'll be in a strange place?' the vet assumed.

Lizzie nodded.

'You're going to have problems, then, because he's unlikely to want to settle. You'd better have some pills to keep him quiet while the leg heals. They'll make him feel drowsy. If he won't accept them directly, put them in his food, or you could even grind them up and dissolve them in warm milk. Don't exceed the dosage on the label. Keep him comfortable and well nourished. Nature should do the rest, providing he accepts you as his friend.'

'I think he already has,' Lizzie said.

She was thoroughly pleased with the vet's diagnosis. She was completely responsible for Sammy's recovery and this meant she could look after him for several weeks. She had no intention of keeping him once he was fit again but she had always wanted a cat and she intended to make the most of it. She hastened back to acquaint Sammy with his new home.

Lizzie lived alone. Her flat was very small. It had a bedroom, a small sitting-room, a bathroom and a tiny kitchen. It was all she could afford. She opened up Sammy's carton, breaking down one side of it so that he could walk or, rather, limp out of it when he should choose. The vet had told her the cat was none too clean and that she should wash him when she thought the time was right. She opened a tin of cat food, put it in a bowl under the kitchen table next to his carton and left Sammy to his own devices whilst she prepared her own meal. The sedative administered to Sammy by the vet had not yet worn off. Lizzie had cooked a simple meal, eaten it, washed up and was relaxing in front of the television before Sammy even stirred. Then out of the corner of her eye, Lizzie saw movement. Sammy had hauled himself to the adjacent food-bowl and was eating. He had fasted for more than twenty-four hours and, despite feeling muzzy, he managed to eat more than half the bowl's contents. Now he moved round to look at his new companion. He saw a slim, pretty young woman of about twenty-six or seven with dark chestnut hair, hazel eyes and the loveliest of human smiles on her face.

'Well – hello, Puss,' said Lizzie. She hadn't yet thought of a proper name for him. 'Welcome to basement life.'

Sammy miaowed at her. He knew she meant to be kind. He had no idea where he was, how he had come there, nor how far he was from Pinkie. One thing he did know. He was entirely in human hands – the hands of the young woman who had tended and fed him.

Lizzie was conscious of the fact that she not only needed to look after Sammy but also the little white cat who was now left on her own. She had seen the cats together in the park enough times to know that they formed a pair. She imagined that life would be more difficult for Pinkie now that she would have to find all her own food. So the next morning Lizzie collected together some scraps to take to the park. She spoke to Sammy while she was doing it.

'You needn't worry about your little friend,' she told him. 'I'll see she doesn't starve while you're not around. Now, let me see, have you got everything *you* need?' As expected, Sammy had refused to take a pill down his throat and had not allowed Lizzie to come near him. So she had ground one up and given it to him in milk. Now Lizzie looked around. 'You've got your bed and your dirt-tray. I know they're strange to you but you'll soon get used to them. You know where your water-bowl is. You've had your milk, so that's all right. I'd perhaps better leave a little food for you because you'll be in all day and you may feel peckish.' She put a small amount of cat food in a saucer, checked the windows were fastened, gave Sammy a reassuring stroke, gathered up her things and left. Sammy, thanks to the tablet, was already feeling torpid. He watched Lizzy go through her routine and he heard the front door bang without realizing what it meant. Alone all day, and in a strange place!

The first day alone Sammy slept most of the time. Lizzie had moved his bed under the window. By the afternoon he felt a little more wakeful. His bad shoulder prevented him from moving around too much and he spent quite a while gazing up at the window that looked out on the road. The pavement was above his head, so he was unable to see more than the lower half of the few people who walked by. However, his interest was aroused when a neighbour's fat black cat strolled up and paused to wash itself on the very stretch of pavement he had been watching. The cat was a male and Sammy instinctively dropped from a sitting position to a crouch. But this was painful and he quickly sat up again. It was odd to see another cat above his head, just as if he were in a tree and the black cat was occupying a higher branch. Sammy stared and stared but the other cat had no idea that it was being observed and eventually strolled on without a glance in his direction. Sammy was relieved, yet disappointed at the same time. He had no other stimulation during the day but what occurred on that piece of pavement. A blackbird perched on the railings outside the house for a brief moment and Sammy chattered at it. But that was all. He ate some of the cat food, drank a drop of water and then curled up in the makeshift bed that Lizzie had made up for him.

It was here that Lizzie found him when she returned from work. She had worried about him all day. Would the tranquillizer work? Or would he panic? Would he aggravate his injury? She could see now from his placid expression that she needn't have concerned herself.

'You look well settled,' she commented. 'I'm so glad. Now I know you'll be quite safe while I'm out. Did you eat anything? Oh yes, I see you did.' Sammy made an effort to rise as she chatted to him. 'No, you stay there and rest,' Lizzie said. 'I'm going to give you something really tasty to eat.' She had bought some calf's liver which she knew would be very good for the invalid Sammy. 'I saw your friend by the lake today,' she went on as she set the liver cooking, 'and I'm afraid she looked very forlorn. She must be missing you. She wouldn't come to me although I tried very hard to persuade her. So I left her some food and watched her from a distance. She was very glad to have it,

I could see. She ate some and carried the rest away. I'll take some more tomorrow. And the weather's going to get much warmer so she'll be just fine.'

The smell of the cooking liver tempted Sammy from his bed and he even managed an awkward totter around Lizzie's legs in the kitchen, rubbing himself against her in the affectionate way he had used in his kitten days with Mrs Lambert.

'Well, well, you look better already,' said Lizzie. 'We're going to get on famously, I can tell. And you'll soon be strong again; you leave it to me. I can't wait for the day when I take you back to the park to re-unite you with that little white female.'

Things went well for over a week. The worst of the winter appeared to be over and a period of balmy weather ensued which certainly had the breath of spring about it. Lizzie faithfully took food to Pinkie though she saw her less and less regularly. She always left the scraps in the same place, well away from greedy seagulls. And Pinkie relied on it. She had given birth to four kittens, one of whom was very weak and had died almost at once. Pinkie always made sure no one was nearby before she collected the food. She wanted no prying eyes to discover her helpless babies. She would take the food back to her den in the stand of bamboo and eat it in peace whilst the kittens suckled. Her dismay at Sammy's disappearance was now almost forgotten in the demanding task of caring for the kittens.

Sammy lived through the days in a sort of semi-doze. He ate well and his injury was mending nicely. He was able to explore the flat more thoroughly in the afternoons when he felt a bit more lively, but he soon found there was nothing much of interest there for him and he always returned to his window on the world, gazing or blinking sleepily at the pavement above. Lizzie was even able to leave him without qualms in the evening when she was out with her boyfriend or visiting her parents or a friend. Sammy was house-trained and for a time he caused her no problems except for a half-hearted struggle when she washed him. After that he kept himself clean.

As he returned to fitness and the pain in his shoulder subsided he was becoming more aware of things. And one of these things was the flavour of the milk which Lizzie religiously set down for him first thing in the morning. The pills she had to give him made the milk taste slightly bitter and, after ten days or so, he grew tired of it and ignored it.

'You mustn't refuse it,' Lizzie admonished him, 'it's helping to make you well. I'll leave it down and I shall be very upset if you haven't drunk it by the time I get home.' She closed the front door with some misgivings but decided there was nothing more she could do for the present.

Sammy resolutely steered clear of the saucer and by midday he was feeling far more spirited. He paced up and down, visiting all the rooms – even the bathroom – and now his shoulder gave him so little trouble that he scarcely limped at all. One each circuit of the flat he paused by the big window in the living-room. He wanted very much to be out there again in the open. He tugged at the outside door with his good foreleg and it didn't, of course, yield. Then he turned his attention to the windows. The kitchen window had no sill so there was nothing he could do there. The bathroom had no window at all, only a ventilator. He wandered into Lizzie's bedroom, his frustration mounting. There was a low sill in this room which he could easily reach because the bed was directly in front of it. Even with his bad shoulder the jump onto the soft bed was easy for him. He got on to the sill and sniffed all along the window. Naturally it was closed fast. He miaowed angrily for a long time, complaining to the empty flat about his lack of freedom. After a while he jumped down again, feeling thirsty. But he walked right past the milk which was beginning to dry up and drank from his water-bowl.

There was still one window he hadn't investigated. He wandered back to the sitting-room. The window-sill was high up. Sammy stared at it with exasperation. He was as good as trapped. Lizzie's flat, although larger, was just as much a prison as the removal van had been. And he seemed to have been here so long! Despite his previously dozed state he was aware of that. He had almost forgotten the park. And what on earth would have happened to Pinkie during all this time? She could have no idea where he was. Was she searching for him? And supposing she was starving. . . . He *must* get out. Sammy growled low in his throat as, just to emphasize his own hopeless position, he saw the fat black cat amble past the windows as free as air.

He weighed up the possibilities of reaching the window-sill. Normally it would have been no problem for him. But dare he risk such a leap after his injury? Well, one thing was certain. If he didn't try he might remain in this place for ever. He crouched, flexing his muscles to test their response. He decided there didn't appear to be too much risk if he could make one big successful bound. As luck would have it the black cat strolled back into Sammy's range of vision as he contemplated his chances. The sight of this sleek animal patrolling the pavement around his prison with the most enviable freedom goaded Sammy into action. He sprang up but, as he launched himself, his injured leg muscles were wrenched and he made a poor job of his jump. His front paws failed to get a grip on the window-sill and the rest of his body thumped against the imprisoning glass before he fell back down to the floor. He landed awkwardly, giving his bad shoulder an excruciating jolt. Sammy howled deafeningly.

The black cat heard the sound and turned to look. It came close up to the railings around the building and peered down at Sammy sprawled on the floor beneath the window. Sammy was furious. His fur rose and he spat at the creature.

'No good swearing at me,' the black cat said loftily. 'Your threats are wasted when you quite obviously can't follow them up.'

'Oh! If I could just get to you!' Sammy roared.

'What's up? Doesn't your mistress trust you?' the black cat teased. He was quite familiar with everyone on his patch and knew exactly who lived where.

'I haven't got any mistress,' Sammy cried. 'I'm in prison and I can't get out. I'm no plumped-up pet like you!'

'A likely story,' the black cat remarked. 'What are you then – a wild animal?'

'I'm my own master,' Sammy growled.

'You certainly look like it, shut up in that poky place,' the black cat said sarcastically.

'Just you wait!'

'Oh, I'll wait as long as you like, Master,' taunted the black cat. 'And when you've decided you dare come out and face me, I'll be ready.' He stepped away with an accentuated nonchalance that maddened Sammy more than the renewed pain that was throbbing through his shoulder and leg. He unsheathed his claws and tore at the carpet with his good paws in fury. His impotency was unbearable.

'Oh, what good is it to be King of the Vagabonds now?' he wailed miserably.

When Lizzie Reed arrived home the first thing she noticed was the untasted milk. Then she saw Sammy's empty bed and finally his food-bowl which also hadn't been touched.

Now she suspected the worst. She ran up to Sammy who was spreadeagled on the floor exactly where he had fallen.

'Oh no!' Lizzie cried. She soon put two and two together – his drowsiness had worn off, he had bcome impatient at being shut in, he had tried to escape and had only succeeded in injuring himself afresh. Sammy looked at her blankly as she fussed around him. Why did she bother? If she really cared about him why didn't she let him go?

Lizzie soon found the scratch marks in her carpet. She didn't have the heart to be angry. She felt sorry for Sammy and wished he could understand that what she was trying to do for him was in his own best interests. She realized he must be very hungry as he hadn't visited his food bowl all day. She went into the kitchen and prepared him some fresh food. She washed his bowl out and then had a brainwave. She could grind a pill up and mix it with the gravy that came out of the tin of cat food.

While she was busy Sammy, who was ravenous, smelt the food she was mixing and hoisted himself to his feet. He limped into the kitchen and miaowed sadly.

'Oh, you're up again!' Lizzie greeted him with relief. 'Perhaps you haven't harmed yourself too much this time. But we can't have a repeat of today. So, there you are.' She plonked his bowl on the floor. 'That should take care of things for now.'

Sammy ate greedily, heedless of the vet's pill amongst the meat. He was soon sleepy again and tottered to his bed. Lizzie sat on the edge of a chair, studying him. She didn't think the idea of administering the pills in his food was such a grand one after all. She could never be sure that, while she was out, he would go to his bowl and eat more than a few morsels. And that wouldn't be enough. It was a pity about the milk because she thought it was more likely he would want a drink. Suddenly, she jumped up.

'I've got it!' she cried. 'I'll take the water-bowl away during the day and then he'll *have* to drink some milk.' She was really pleased with this idea because, now that Sammy had set himself back, it was likely he would have to stay in the flat for a few more weeks. Lizzie did think she had rid herself of a difficulty but then she had reckoned without the interference of a certain fat black cat.

— 5 —

Escape

Pinkie's kittens were growing fast. She was occasionally able to leave them long enough to go hunting to supplement the diet of scraps provided by Lizzie. Pinkie wasn't as strong nor as adept a hunter as Sammy. Duck were beyond her but she could still pin down a pigeon, and small birds such as sparrows or starlings were comparatively easy. She would carry her catch back to her den and her little tabby and white kittens would cluster around her, hungry and demanding. Pinky could see Sammy in every one of them and at times she felt sad. She couldn't understand why he had abandoned her and she still expected him to return to her one day. Then what a surprise and a welcome he would have! But, with the kittens nestling about her, she would soon forget him again in her need to remain watchful and protective towards her little ones.

She gave them names. The male she called Little Sammy after his father. The female kittens she called Moss and Fern in memory of Quartermile Field. 'Your father would be so proud of you,' Pinkie told them over and over again. 'One day he'll come to see you and when he does he won't want to stray again. We'll all live here together until it's time to go home.' She continued to think in terms of going back to Quartermile Field, although quite how this was to be accomplished she didn't begin to know. She believed they would find a way when Sammy returned. In the meantime the weather steadily improved and there were no alarms, other than Sammy's absence to worry about.

But things were changing. In the milder weather the frozen ground thawed. The frost and ice turned to water. Everything in the park became sopping wet and underfoot the park was marshy, with a coating of slimy mud. To make matters worse it rained frequently. Pinkie found it increasingly difficult to keep the kittens dry. The bamboo shrubbery was thick and almost impenetrable but the leaves dripped and Pinkie's den grew wetter and wetter. She herself lost her prettiness. She was no longer white and her fur was never dry. She tried to shield the youngsters from the incessant dripping with her body, but when she left them to collect food there was no way she could protect them. She would come back to find the three of them all in a huddle, miserable, matted and mewling plaintively.

'Oh, poor kittens, poor tiny kittens, what am I going to do?' Pinkie wailed as she licked them vigorously with a rasping tongue. 'I must find something better for you, I don't know where.'

The waterbirds irritated her tremendously. Their enjoyment of the conditions as they dipped and splashed in the lake, cackling and screeching to each other, drew nothing but contempt from Pinkie. 'Stupid, stupid birds,' she growled at them.

'I must look elsewhere,' Pinkie told herself. 'The kittens will perish if we stay here. Oh Sammy, where are you? We need a shelter. But how can I leave here before you get back?'

Sammy's forced captivity dragged on. If he hadn't

attempted his acrobatics his shoulder would have healed itself and he would have been close to release. Now he had condemned himself to a longer period in Lizzie Reed's flat. But he didn't know that.

For some days he went back to drinking his milk because there was no water. He didn't enjoy it; it tasted as strange as before. Then he'd fall asleep below the living-room window and usually only woke up if there was a loud noise outside or if he was hungry. Every so often the black cat would return to the pavement overlooking Sammy's prison and voice a taunt or two for amusement. However, as long as Sammy drank the milk, he didn't hear him.

Eventually Lizzie came to the end of the pills the vet had given her and she rang up to enquire if the cat would need any more. She was told that the treatment should not be continued, that Sammy's injuries should have healed by now, and that he should be well on the way to a complete recovery. Lizzie explained about the new injury. The vet said it was unfortunate but not entirely un-expected since a feral cat was bound to chafe at its confinement and would want to escape. He suggested Lizzie put a lead on him and take him outside now and then to explore.

'I don't know if that will work,' said Lizzie. 'He's rather wild and he wouldn't enjoy being on a leash. But I'll try anyway.'

Yet there never seemed to be an opportunity when it wasn't raining. The first weekend that came along was wet and dismal. Sammy was a little less frustrated when Lizzie was around because she spoke to him and fussed over him. But when Monday came and he was left alone once more he couldn't contain himself.

He ate his food during the first half-hour of Lizzie's absence. Then he looked around for something else to do. He sharpened his claws on the kitchen door. His claws scythed across the painted wood, leaving deep scratches. His leg, he was sure, was healed. He ran into the bathroom, intrigued by the sound of a dripping tap. The water didn't hold his interest for long. He jumped down from the bath without a mishap, ran into the living-room and skidded to a halt by the window. The black cat, taking advantage of a lull between showers, was staring down into the flat.

'Don't tell me you *still* haven't found the way out?' he sneered at Sammy. 'What do you do all day?'

A low growl began in Sammy's throat but he didn't answer.

'I've seen you,' the black cat teased, 'curled up like a kitten with your head on your tail. You ought to sleep a bit less, you might find out something!'

'You'd better not say any more, Fatty,' Sammy warned him in a voice harsh and menacing, 'or you'll live to regret it.'

The black cat grinned a cat grin. 'What are you going to do, Master Sleeper? Try and dream your way out of here?'

The cat's contempt was the last straw for Sammy. His claws tore at the carpet, but it was too tough to yield much to his exasperation. He turned his attention to the settee and attacked the cushions, tearing strips out of them. After that he paused, his temper only a little cooled by his effort. 'I'm going to get that fat self-satisfied animal,' he swore to himself. 'And it's going to be tonight.'

When it was early evening he positioned himself by the front door and waited impatiently. The rain poured down outside, flooding the pavements and road. Sammy didn't care a jot. At last he heard Lizzie's footsteps and he made ready for flight. The key was in the door; it turned; the door opened. Sammy dashed out as if he had been fired from a gun. In the darkness the startled Lizzie didn't even see where he went.

'Oh Puss!' she cried. 'Come back, you don't know where you are.' She gave a little sob. She knew the very last thing Sammy would do would be to come back. He was gone for good, and into a strange environment where he could never hope to find his little white companion again. She shut the front door with a tearful expression. It was a while before her tears allowed her to discover the destruction wrought by Sammy's temper.

Sammy's main concern all day had been to teach the black cat a lesson. Of course now, in this downpour, he was nowhere about. Sammy's priority, therefore, became to find shelter. He sprinted under the nearest parked car, muttering to himself, 'The weather won't save you, Fat Cat.'

Under the car he had time to reflect. Pinkie came quickly into his thoughts. How was she coping in these unpleasant conditions? Once he had redressed the taunts of his neighbour he must get back to her. But how? Sammy pondered.

Across the road were some tall railings. There were no houses on that side. Sammy saw emptiness and a blackness deeper than the sky, a blackness that reflected the lights from street lamps and lighted windows, making the reflections bob and ripple in the rain. He was looking at the Regent's Canal.

When the rain slackened to a softer beat Sammy moved. He ambled across the deserted road. The water fascinated him. It stretched in either direction as far as his eye could reach. A chord was struck in his memory. He remembered the stretch of water along the edge of the park. This looked remarkably similar. He began to believe that, like the stream near his old home in Quartermile Field, this water could lead him back to Pinkie and his previous haunts in the park. But first he had to deal with the black cat. . . .

Sammy had the advantage of surprise. The other cat would be thinking he was still in the flat. There was nothing to be done now. It was night-time and the black cat was nowhere around. Sammy contented himself with a little exploration. His instinct told him which direction to take along the canal side and, even though he only walked a short distance, he could feel unmistakably that he was walking towards Pinkie. The pavement sloped up to a junction. Here the road was crossed by a much wider and busier one. The canal ran underneath this road. So· Sammy knew he'd have to cross it to regain the waterside. He watched the traffic. It didn't seem too daunting. He turned and padded back towards Lizzie's flat. He sat on the pavement outside her living-room window and looked down at what had been his prison. Lizzie had pulled the curtains and Sammy gazed at the yellow rectangle of light. It was a strange feeling to be outside the very place where he had so often sat looking upwards with such intense frustration.

He passed the rest of the night alternately ambling and resting. When daylight returned he hid under a car and waited for Lizzie to leave the flat. He was surprised to see her come out carrying a plate of food. She looked up and down the road as if uncertain where to place it. Finally, she opted for a spot against the railings by the canal. Sammy watched her walk away. She turned her head frequently, always hoping to catch a glimpse of the tabby cat she had sheltered and whom, uncannily, she believed to be still in the vicinity. But Sammy stayed hidden.

'What a kind person she has been,' Sammy mused. 'I haven't repaid her very well for her kindness, although I did *try* to be friendly. Even now I've escaped from her she still thinks about me. If only she hadn't kept me shut in all the time. We *could* have been friends, good friends. I don't really understand humans.'

Lizzie disappeared and Sammy crept from his hiding-place to examine what she had left him. There was a generous portion of tinned meat on the plate. He had some thoughts of leaving it. He had made the break from her care, but he knew if he didn't eat it another animal would, and immediately he was reminded of the black cat.

'Mustn't waste it,' Sammy murmured to himself. 'I shall need all my strength.'

When he had finished the meat Sammy stood for a moment licking his chops. He licked a paw and washed his face. Because of the good food provided for him over the past few weeks he felt generally fitter and stronger than he had since the summer. Of course there was his shoulder injury but that gave him very little pain now. He felt ready for anything. He watched a couple of cars pass and then strolled back across the road. It was a fine, clear, bright morning. It was simply a matter of waiting for the black cat to appear.

Sammy knew where he lived. He had followed his scent during the night to the next house but one. He had gone right up to the front door where the scent had been very strong. And he had listened. The animal's voice, responding to its owner's, had been easily detectable from within. Sammy watched the front door now. After just a short while it opened. The black cat came out, stretched, yawned and sauntered down the path to the pavement. Sammy stole back underneath the parked car. He was tense and excited. The black cat turned and walked towards Lizzie's flat. It stopped outside and Sammy knew it was relishing another opportunity to taunt him. He crept out from the car and sat down quickly behind the animal's black back. The cat sensed something was there. Its head turned. Sammy smiled a cat smile.

'So – we're on equal terms now,' said the tabby. 'Both on street level. I'm sorry to deprive you of your source of fun.'

The black cat swallowed hard. Its tail swished and it glanced to one side as though weighing up the possibilities of flight. 'How did you –?' it began.

'Escape? Easy. I stopped sleeping and made a plan. And now I *am* my own master again.'

'What – what do you intend to do?' the black cat murmured. It was very nervous.

'Oh – get even, just as I promised,' Sammy replied coolly. 'So come on, Fat Cat. Let's see what overfed pets are made of round here.' He remained motionless, waiting for the other animal's first move which he guessed would be an attempt to run away.

'I – er – haven't any particular quarrel,' the black cat ventured to say. 'You mistook me. I was only joking with you before. Wouldn't it be better to forget your grievances?'

'That's not how I see it,' Sammy growled. 'Come on, coward, make me move.'

The black cat was riled by the insult. It hissed at Sammy. Then Sammy sprang forward and the two cats tussled, biting and clawing at each other furiously. The black cat was heavy but Sammy very soon knew that it had no real fighting ability. He bundled it over on to its back and held it down with teeth and four sets of claws. The black cat trembled. It hadn't imagined this tabby could have proved so savage. Sammy was like a young tiger. He seemed to have the strength of two animals. All fight and pride went out of the black cat and it waited for Sammy to decide its fate. For a few moments Sammy retained his crushing grip. Then suddenly he relaxed.

'Pah! You're not worth bothering with,' he spat with the most supreme contempt. 'Get up and go back to your cosy home and pampered lifestyle. And make sure you tell the other softies on your patch that Sammy, King of the Vagabonds, is about and to steer clear of his path. You see, I'm free to travel where I want to now and I don't want anyone to get in my way.'

The black cat ran without a word, expecting every moment to find the tabby on its tail. But Sammy had no intention of following it. He'd taught the creature a lesson and reckoned that, if all the cats dwelling in this type of environment were as sleek and plump as that one, he, Sammy, could already count himself as being without challenge.

—6—

Toby

However, Sammy had misled himself. Not all the animals in the city environment were spoilt pets – far from it. But he was yet to find this out. Pinkie had already attracted the interest of one of these other city dwellers who, like Sammy, called themselves their own masters.

It had happened like this. Pinkie had been determined to find drier quarters for the kittens. Moss, Fern and Little Sammy were looking more and more bedraggled day by day and Pinkie found it impossible to keep herself clean. One evening, out of desperation, she left the kittens mewing on their saturated bedding and left the park by the entrance where she and Sammy had first come in. She was certain there must be somewhere better, somewhere drier, amongst all those clustered buildings, where she could make a snug home for her little family. She didn't think any of the kittens would reach adulthood unless she moved them.

The buildings that backed on to the park each had a garden or yard. Some of these gardens were maintained, others were wildernesses. In one of these yards connected to a shop, the owners had disposed of all the unwanted boxes and cartons that came into their premises. These were piled up in a corner underneath a sheet of corrugated iron attached to the wall, and were mostly dry. In her exploration of the yards, Pinkie came to this one quite soon and was very excited. Any one of the boxes offered a perfect shelter for her and the kittens where they could keep dry and comparatively warm. Some of them had packing materials such as straw or paper inside. The yard seemed to be quiet enough, she observed. She hesitated no longer. There was everything she wanted here. The spot was even close enough to the park to enable her to bring food back for the kittens when they grew bigger. She ran back through the darkness to the bamboo shrubbery to fetch the first of the kittens.

She found them all safe. She picked up Moss by the scruff of her neck and slowly, carrying the kitten in her mouth, she made the return journey. Moss hung limp and passive against her mother's chest as Pinkie ran. A kitten will do this instinctively when carried, to enable the parent cat to move away from danger with the least difficulty and with maximum speed. Pinkie deposited Moss in the chosen box and raced back for the second kitten. Fern was soon on her way to join her sister. Pinkie was leaving the yard for the third time to pick up her last kitten when a strange voice spoke to her out of the darkness.

'I've been watching you. How many more have you got to bring? I could help, you know.'

Pinkie froze as she tried to locate the owner of the voice.

'Up here. On the wall,' she was told.

She looked up. A burly-looking grey tom with eyes that gleamed green in the moonlight hugged the wall coping as he stared down at her.

'Have – have you been there all the time?' Pinkie whispered, very much on her guard.

'You haven't noticed me?' the male cat asked with surprise. 'I've been watching you. It'll be nice for old Toby to have a bit of company.'

'Toby? Company?' Pinkie echoed, uncertain of her next move. 'Do you – live here?' She dreaded the answer. She wanted no strange tom near her kittens.

'Hereabouts,' he answered cheerily. 'It's a good spot, isn't it? We all need dry quarters. Be just right for you and your little 'uns.'

'Are you Toby?' Pinkie answered with a sinking heart. She didn't know whether to fetch Little Sammy or to take the other kittens back to the bamboo thicket. Which was safer now?

'That's me,' replied the tom in answer to her question. 'And who are you? You're a bit special. I haven't seen anyone quite so quick and nimble as you for a long while,' he added.

Pinkie was almost flattered. But she was in a dilemma. She couldn't risk leaving Little Sammy any longer on his own. Yet would his sisters be secure when she turned her back?

'I have another one to bring,' she murmured. 'I daren't leave him alone any longer. I must go.' Then she had an idea. 'His father's gone hunting,' she fibbed. 'He may be back by now and he may not.' She thought the tom would be more cautious if he believed another male was around.

'You fetch the youngster,' Toby told her. 'I'll keep guard while Father's not around.' He didn't sound in the least concerned.

Pinkie knew she must go. There was no help for it. She must simply hope this Toby was to be trusted.

'You haven't told me who you are,' the grey tom reminded her.

'I'm called Pinkie,' she said. She took a last look at Moss and Fern and then vanished.

Toby jumped down from the wall and stepped over to the kittens' new nursery. They were already settling themselves amongst the straw. When the strange cat's big round face peered into the box they backed away, making little hissing sounds. Toby was amused. 'What a fuss,' he commented. 'I'm quite harmless, you know. Just standing guard whilst your mother goes for the other one. We'd make a good pair, don't you think?' He sat down by the side of the box muttering, 'Toby and Pinkie, Pinkie and Toby. Father's away hunting. . . . ha ha, I know better than that.'

Minutes later Pinkie was back. Little Sammy was heavier than his sisters and she was tired. She quickly checked that Moss and Fern were safe. They were asleep but they woke up when Little Sammy was introduced to the box.

'It seems you were true to your word,' Pinkie remarked, glancing at Toby who was sitting rather like a sentry next to the box.

'Of course, why should you have doubted it?'

'Well, we're strangers, aren't we? How could I be sure?'

'Hm. You certainly took a risk then, if you *weren't* sure, leaving them in such an exposed position.' He indicated the kittens. 'And besides, we're not such strangers really, Pinkie. At least, I don't think of you as a stranger.'

'Why, what do you mean?'

'Oh, I've been keeping my eye on you for some time. I've seen you about in the park, usually near the lake. I've been admiring the grace and delicacy with which you go about finding food. I'm delighted we're going to be companions.'

Pinkie gaped. This cat had watched her in the park! How was it she had never seen him? She didn't like the way he was insinuating himself into her company. She hadn't asked for it.

'I don't think we can be companions – ever,' she said. 'I have my kittens to look after and you – you have *your* life.'

'Nonsense,' Toby purred, 'we'll just be like one happy

family, you wait and see.' His voice had taken on a barely detectable harsher note. But Pinkie had noticed it.

'We couldn't possibly be like a family,' she assured him coolly. Her temper was kindled and it gave her courage. 'You can't have two adult males in a family of cats.'

'Two?' Toby queried. 'Two toms?' He pretended to be mystified. 'Where's the other one?'

'I told you the kittens' father was out hunting,' Pinkie said. Now there was an edge to her voice. 'You see, I have a mate – Sammy.'

'Oh-ho, come now, Pinkie. I wasn't born yesterday. There's no Sammy or any other mate. Not any more. If there were I'd have seen him, wouldn't I? I can't blame you for trying but really, how many toms stay around in one place for long, with one mate? Especially when there are kittens! It's just not in our nature. Sammy's gone, hasn't he? You're on your own – or you *were*.'

Pinkie was silent. Her tail swished. She was angry, yet she was, in a way, caught. Sammy wasn't around any more. That much was true. But she objected strongly to this animal's assumption that he was going to take Sammy's place. She daren't risk upsetting the grey tom in case the kittens were to pay the penalty for it. He was quite capable of doing them harm if she tried to thwart him. So it would be best to play along for now and then take the first opportunity to get away from here with the kittens. She realized with a pang that the park could no longer be considered a safe haven. She looked steadily at Toby.

'What do you want from me?' she enquired.

'Why, I told you,' he answered. 'Your company!' He knew she was in a corner. 'Your company and your – co-operation,' he finished, leaving Pinkie to make up her own mind what *that* meant.

Pinkie gave a low growl. 'I suppose I can't avoid your company,' she said. 'But I can't answer for the consequences when Sammy comes back.'

'Don't you mean *if* he comes back?' Toby asked subtly. 'It's perfectly obvious you don't know where he is.'

Pinkie didn't say any more. She got into the box she had chosen and the kittens settled themselves against her. She purred. This place was beautifully dry and snug, so much better than the muddy park.

'A picture of contentment,' Toby remarked wryly.

Yes, thought Pinkie. It would be that, if only *you* weren't around.

Pinkie and her little family didn't stir from the box during the rest of the night. The grey tom wandered away when they were all sleeping. By morning the kittens and Pinkie were quite dry. She gave Moss, Fern and Little Sammy a thorough washing, then she set about her own coat. Her fur began to look something like its true white colour again. Pinkie was relieved to see that Toby was nowhere in evidence.

'It's a pity I've got to move away from here when we've only just made ourselves comfortable,' she said to the kittens. 'I really think we must go, though. I don't like strange cats coming around us uninvited.' She stopped speaking as she heard noises coming from the shop to which the yard was attached. She pricked up her ears. A door in the rear of the premises was opened and a man stepped out. He called back to someone who was inside. Pinkie tensed. 'Quickly, hide yourselves,' she hissed to the kittens. She hustled them deeper into the straw until they were more or less covered by it. Then she slunk away from the box in order to make it less conspicuous. She secreted herself behind a pile of cartons and waited until all was quiet again.

Suddenly, a voice she recognized said, 'I'm flattered. How did you know to find me here?' It was Toby whose grey head she now saw peeping from the flap of one of the cartons.

'I wasn't looking for *you*,' Pinkie declared irritably. 'People are about and I didn't want to lead them to the kittens.'

'Oh, now I'm disappointed,' said Toby with a cat grin. He of course knew this quite well.

'Don't be ridiculous,' Pinkie said scathingly. 'I haven't any inclination to listen to your nonsense.'

Toby's eyes glinted. 'But you must listen to me!' he snapped so sharply that Pinkie was startled. He went on in smoother tones. 'It's part of being a companion, isn't it?'

Pinkie said nothing for a while, then she asked, 'Is that where you sleep, in that thing?'

'Here or another, it's all the same to me,' the tom told her.

'How long have you lived here?'

'Long enough to know loneliness.'

Pinkie blinked. Toby sounded different – subdued. 'Are there other cats on your territory?'

'There was one,' Toby said softly. 'She was lovely. She looked very like you – glossy white fur, smart, and fast on her feet.'

'What happened to her?'

'She was killed. Run over on that busy road.' He indicated the road Sammy and Pinkie had crossed to get to the park. 'She wasn't very old. She was running to join me and the next minute she was struck and tossed into the air. It was a horrible thing to see.'

Pinkie looked sympathetically at the tom. She guessed that the white cat had once been his mate. She also guessed that he was looking to her to act as a substitute. Before she could comment Toby continued. 'That's why I used to come and watch you, you see. You reminded me so much of her.'

'I understand,' Pinkie said quietly. 'Actually I – *we*,' she hastily amended, 'we don't come from these parts.'

'I thought as much,' Toby said. 'You talk differently – with an accent. Tell me about yourself.'

Pinkie related how she and Sammy had arrived in the city unexpectedly and she described her old home and the life she had known amongst the vagabond cats.

Toby listened without interruption. 'It was the same here when I was young,' he said afterwards. 'Lots of animals. But most of them were rounded up by the humans and taken away. I think there were just too many and they didn't like that.'

'You survived.'

'Yes. Oh yes. I'm the great survivor.'

'Are you content here?'

'No. That is, I *may* be now,' he said meaningfully.

Pinkie quickly changed the subject. 'I want to go back to my home,' she said, 'but I don't know how to do it. It seems so far away.'

'Your first duty is to your youngsters,' Toby remarked.

'Of course it is. They need me and I must get back to them now. There's no danger at the moment and they'll need feeding.' She paused. 'Er – I'm glad you told me about yourself,' she said. 'I understand better now.'

'Good. You know, I can help you–' Toby repeated, 'with feeding, and other things too.'

'Feeding? How can you?'

'I know where there's plenty of meat. I'll show you. There's a place where humans fetch their own meat. At the back the man throws a lot of it away. Come with me now, we'll bring some back.'

'My babies don't eat meat yet,' Pinkie said with some amusement at Toby's eagerness. 'They're still suckling.'

'But you – you're not a great hunter,' he observed. 'I've seen you collecting the scraps. *You* could benefit.'

'I could,' admitted Pinkie.

'Well then?'
'Wait for me here. I'll return as soon as I can.'

Along the canal

Ignorant of everything that had affected Pinkie's life, Sammy was on his way back to the park. He took the route along the canalside and once more reached the crossroads he had examined the night before. In the daytime the constant stream of nose-to-tail traffic made it impossible to continue. To attempt a crossing in the rush hour would be to invite almost certain death. He was forced to bide his time. He wandered up and down the road. If Lizzie Reed had been home she would have been astonished to discover just how close to her flat Sammy had remained. The black cat kept out of sight but every time Sammy passed its house he adopted a sort of swagger, as though to vaunt his superiority. He was in danger of his vanity making him careless. He remembered his other conquests back in Quartermile Field – of Brindle, and the strong ginger cat Sunny who had hated him, and then of the king cat, Brute, whose relationship to himself he hadn't understood until after their fight. He had conquered them all. He was a great fighter and he feared nothing except what he had recently experienced – a loss of freedom.

Later in the morning, Sammy returned to the cross-roads. The tabby was eager to get back to Pinkie. He recalled how he had crossed that other road. There were now occasional lapses in the motor traffic. When it was quiet Sammy shot forward. The road was clear. Then, from a side turning, a cyclist swung out without warning. In the middle of the road Sammy froze. He had good cause to fear bicycles. It was the worst thing he could have done. Once more the traffic bore down in both directions. Sammy couldn't go back and he couldn't go on. He was stuck between lanes, a tiny forlorn figure dwarfed by roaring metal monsters on either side. As they whizzed past, drivers glanced curiously at the cowering cat. But nobody stopped. Passers-by, unable to enter the mêlée, clapped hands to mouths in horror of the seemingly inevitable ghastly end to the cat's predicament. But Sammy was a lucky cat. Almost level with where he was crouching a huge lorry squealed to a halt. The driver leapt out and ran round to the back, holding up his hands to the vehicles behind. Amid a barrage of hoots and shouts Sammy bolted to the other side of the road, completely unharmed.

Without a second thought, Sammy careered along the pavement, tail flying, dodging people and dogs, and hugging a wall or fence wherever he could, eager to put as much distance as possible between himself and his terrifying experience. He kept a straight course past houses and a corner shop, always in the direction of Pinkie. But, when he was sufficiently calm to notice, he realized that his guide and pointer, the canal, seemed to have disappeared. How could Sammy know that this stretch of the canal was built over, that there was no towpath for him to follow?

He paused at the end of the road of terraced houses, opposite a large and busy pub. The air was mild and suddenly the unmistakable smell of stagnant water wafted across to him. That was the smell he was searching for! He recognized it instantly from the canal reach opposite Lizzie's flat. Sammy sniffed and followed the scent. For a while it didn't get any stronger but, as he rounded a corner by a block of flats, the full rich ripe scent of the dark water assailed him. He edged forward, stepping circumspectly, and there below him was the familiar serpentine wind of the canal. Sammy bounded down some wooden stairs, then some steps to the canalside path. A lone jogger ran towards him from the distance.

Sammy was sure now that if he kept to the waterside he must eventually come to the park. He knew this could prove to be a long journey but the path looked empty and free from danger. He must find food where he could on the way. He concentrated his thoughts on Pinkie. Would she still be in the park? What if the strange wild animals had discovered her? Oh, what was he going to find when he got back? It was so long since he had seen her and so much could have happened.

As the jogger approached, Sammy took the precaution of hiding himself in a mass of weeds that grew against a high wall on his left. He needn't have bothered. The track-suited man didn't even give him a glance. Sammy remained sitting for a moment.

'How peaceful it is here,' he said to himself, remembering the din and rush of motor traffic. 'I don't think there will be much to hinder me along the way. But I must steer clear of humans, I can't afford to get trapped again.' He jumped clear of the weeds, amongst whose dead stalks new growth was already beginning to show, and went forward again. Now, the path was entirely devoid of people. Occasionally a sparrow or two alighted on the path and hopped about, in search of seeds or crumbs. Sammy was eager to practise his hunting techniques after such a long period of dependency. Each time he saw the birds he squatted and watched. If they stayed around long enough he began to slink forward, hopeful of reviving his old skills. The sparrows never remained on the ground for more than a few moments. They were supremely wary of any sort of movement. Sammy was unable to come anywhere near them.

'They must know I'm fast,' he told himself to compensate. 'They'll know all about cats, that's for sure. And if they're cagey about the pets round here, they'll need to be especially heedful of an expert like me. Oh, I'd like to show them!' Sammy snarled, picturing himself stalking rabbits back in the overgrown allotments near Quartermile Field.

The path stretched ahead several hundred metres and then disappeared into a short tunnel. Sammy's progress was rapid, broken only by the periodic interruptions of the sparrows. The darkness of the tunnel didn't alarm him. It was still light enough in there to see everything he needed to see – what was ahead of him, what was behind him, what was approaching on the canal – and indeed he saw absolutely nothing to disturb him. He did see boats but none of them moved.

They were houseboats, moored in a line against the near bank. People lived on them. Some of the occupants had made little gardens of flowers along the border by the footpath. Nobody was stirring just then but Sammy sensed their presence and he slunk along stealthily, careful not to arouse any interest. However, there were not only people living on the houseboats. A small brown mongrel, not unlike a Staffordshire terrier, had been dozing on deck on one of the craft. He awoke as Sammy stole past. He jumped up, instantly alert, and yapped.

'Hey – you! Wait!' The dog strained at a short chain secured to the deck. 'Don't run!'

Sammy hesitated. He looked across at the dog and saw that the animal was restricted by its chain. He relaxed. 'What do you want?' he asked.

The dog replied with a question. 'Can you catch mice?' it demanded unexpectedly.

'Of course I can catch mice,' Sammy answered indignantly.

'*Any* sort of mice?'

'What sort of mice are there? They're all the same.'

The dog disagreed. 'Oh no,' it said, 'they're not at all. Perhaps you're not such a great mouser after all, if you think that.'

Sammy was becoming impatient. 'Look, what's all this about? I haven't got time to waste, I'm on my way back home.'

'All right, I'll tell you,' said the dog. 'You see this chain?' He turned and snapped viciously at it as if it were a live thing. 'I've been attached to this hateful object as a punishment because I *can't* catch mice – or, at any rate, not one particular one. But a cat now – that's different.'

Sammy was interested despite himself. 'Cats *are* different,' he concurred, 'especially where mice are concerned.'

'Yes. Well, my mistress hates them. She's got a thing about mice. They bother her where she goes to work. I've been there. Mice everywhere. It's in an old building, you see. Mice love those, don't they? And now there's one on this boat. Oh, and it's so clever! I was set to catch it – and failed. The commotion it caused! I tried everything and I did do my best. What a fuss. Now I'm out here in disgrace and my mistress is refusing to feed me. I think she thinks if I get hungry enough I'll be more determined to catch the mouse.' The dog broke off to give a howl of misery. 'I shall *never* catch it,' it resumed. 'I'm called Smartie but I'm not smart enough for this mouse. It's too quick and nimble for me. I just crash into things and upset everything. And it's so cheeky! It pinches food right in front of your eyes and then it sits and laughs at you. I'll never get it, never,' the dog moaned. 'I'll starve first. I know I will.'

Sammy began to understand where he fitted into this

business. And he was tempted. 'You want me to have a try, I suppose?' he enquired diffidently, stretching his legs.

'You've got it!'

'Where's your mistress now?'

'In the galley – er – seeing to things.'

'Seeing to things?'

'Well, clearing up actually. I caused a bit of a mess.'

'In the chase?'

'Yes.'

'You dogs are so clumsy,' Sammy remarked. 'No finesse. No stealth. Not like a cat.'

The dog encouraged him. 'Exactly,' it said. 'Cats are smooth operators. Er – you look pretty smooth, Cat. What's your name?'

'Sammy.'

'Look, Sammy, can you help? Jump on board.'

Sammy obliged.

'You fix this mouse for good,' said Smartie, coming up close and giving him the once-over. 'You look lithe and fit. I know we never saw each other before today but, will you have a go? I'm desperate. I want to be fed.'

'What do I get out of it?' Sammy asked subtly.

'My undying friendship,' Smartie replied.

Sammy's tail twitched. He was undecided. He had quite taken to this animal who was honest and friendly, if nothing else. But how long would it take? He didn't want to lose a lot of time hunting on another's behalf. On the other hand, this mouse was a challenge; there was no doubt about it. His vanity was tickled and he forgot his earlier scruples about human contact. 'All right then,' he said. 'I'll do it.'

Smartie barked exultantly.

'Where do I go?'

'Down there,' the dog indicated. 'Into the cabin. The

mouse could be anywhere. But *you'll* smell it out, eh?'

'Undoubtedly,' Sammy boasted. 'Only a matter of time.'

'Give the mistress a greeting,' Smartie suggested. 'She's not expecting you and she'll like that.'

Sammy descended the few steps. Smartie, at the full extent of his chain, watched him go. A quick kill, thought Sammy, and then on my way again.

He paused at the bottom of the stairway. A middle-aged woman, well-built with hair turning to grey, was on her hands and knees in the galley sweeping up broken crockery and the spilt contents of several food containers. She was muttering angrily to herself. 'One mouse and all this chaos! Oh if I could just catch the little. . .' She broke off as she saw Sammy peering at her. He seemed to be the answer to a prayer.

'Well! Would you believe it? Where have you come from?'

Sammy miaowed at her politely.

'This is timely, Elsie,' the woman addressed herself, and with some difficulty hauled herself on to her feet, whilst making friendly clucking noises to the tabby cat who watched her. At the top of the steps Smartie waved his tail slowly from side to side. 'You look a bit wild,' the woman commented next, 'but that's all to the good.'

Sammy wasn't afraid. Her friendly tones reassured him. He continued to watch her and, as he did so, he saw a quick movement behind her. A mouse – *the* mouse, he guessed – was scurrying across the floor carrying a fragment of biscuit between its tiny jaws. Sammy froze. His eyes left the woman's face and switched to the mouse, following its progress as it began to climb up the leg of a chair. This was indeed a bold mouse and one that needed to be taught a lesson. It seemed that the mouse intended to climb on to the table where perhaps it believed it would be able to eat its biscuit with more ease. It hadn't noticed the tabby cat so still and tense in the corner. Sammy decided to forestall it. He ran forward and leapt up on to the table-top. As the mouse came into view he was ready for it. He pounced just as the mouse reached the level of the table and, with great accuracy, trapped it between his paws. The woman shrieked with a mixture of surprise and excitement. Her tormentor was caught!

Sammy didn't wait for congratulations. With the mouse lifeless in his mouth he leapt down from the table and headed for the steps up to deck. Smartie barked with delight.

'Amazing, amazing,' he yapped as Sammy deposited the carcass before him as proof of his skills. 'I wouldn't have believed you could be so speedy. I bet you've earned your own dinner as well as mine.'

Sammy was set to spurn this offer when he heard the woman's heavy footsteps approach from behind.

'What a treasure,' she crooned to him as she bent and lifted him into her arms. 'If you can catch one mouse you can catch more and I know just the place where you can find them.'

It was useless for Sammy to struggle. The woman was powerful and she held him tight against her bosom. Smartie frisked about joyfully. The woman carried Sammy down to the cabin again. 'You're just what we need in that rickety old building with all its nooks and holes,' Sammy was told. 'An instinctive mouser!'

—8—

Miles apart

Pinkie was ready to join Toby the grey tom to fetch food. She had satisfied herself that her kittens were well fed and warm. Then she covered them over, telling them she would be back very soon.

Toby waited for her on the wall coping. 'Hungry?' he asked. '*I* am.'

Pinkie *was* hungry. She hadn't been to see if Lizzie's scraps were in their usual place in the park. She followed Toby along the crest of the wall without further ado. They came to a butcher's yard. Pinkie's nostrils had long since caught the rich fatty scent of raw meat.

'We have to be on our guard from now on,' Toby told her. 'We may not be the only ones looking to fill our stomachs.'

Pinkie glanced at him sharply. 'I thought you said there weren't any other cats?' she snapped.

'No cats, no. But there are other animals. There's a big black dog who comes here sometimes. He has a huge head and jaws and great long legs. He can jump like anything. He comes from the park and leaps over this wall. And he doesn't tolerate competition. Many's the time I've had to run for my life.'

Pinkie glared. 'Why didn't you warn me before?'

'I thought you wouldn't come,' Toby answered

honestly. 'And the dog doesn't often make an appearance. Believe me, it's worth taking the chance. You'll understand when you see what's on offer.'

'Who else comes, apart from the black dog?' Pinkie demanded.

'Er – well, I sometimes see a couple of smaller dogs. But they're no problem. They're not fierce. They're pets who are sometimes let out on their own.'

'The black dog isn't a pet, of course,' Pinkie remarked with irony.

'I should say not. Humans generally don't keep fierce animals, do they, except to guard themselves? No, he walks on his own, that one.'

'Well, that *is* reassuring,' Pinkie continued sarcastically. 'So we're likely to be heading towards a throng of dogs and, if we're not, then this black monster could turn up anywhere, anytime, even while we're innocently asleep.'

'Don't be silly,' said Toby. 'He's only interested in the food. If you don't meddle with him you've nothing to fear. Now, follow me.' He jumped down from the wall and, raising his head, tested the air for dog odours. 'All clear,' he announced.

The yard was paved. It was empty of animal life. There were clusters of black plastic sacks tied at the neck, all of which smelt strongly – and some rankly – of meat and offal. Toby strolled across to the nearest bunch, keeping his eyes and ears on full alert. He paused and sniffed at the sacks, one after another. 'They tear easily,' he commented. He unsheathed his claws and dug them into the plastic. A hole instantly appeared in the sack which Toby quickly enlarged. 'There's some liver here,' he told Pinkie. 'Quite fresh too.'

Pinkie's mouth watered. She sat a metre or so away.

Every so often she turned her head back to the wall, expecting to see a giant black dog bounding over it.

'There are some meaty bones too,' Toby went on. He put his grey head right inside the hole and pulled out some lumps of liver. 'Here – take some,' he offered Pinkie.

Pinkie came up and, with yet another glance behind her, began to eat. The liver tasted good. Toby pulled out some more. There were some sausages and lamb bones.

'Best not to eat much of it here,' he advised. 'Find a safe place and–' He broke off abruptly and swivelled his head round. 'I think I heard something – a bark!' he hissed. 'Grab what you can and come with me.'

Pinkie took a large piece of liver between her teeth and Toby grabbed a string of six sausages. He ran to the back of the yard, sausages trailing behind him. Pinkie was hard on his tail. They leapt up to the top of the wall. Toby led Pinkie along to the greengrocer's yard next door. An enormous ivy plant grew in the corner, draping the wall like a cloak. Toby let his sausages hang down amongst the tendrils. 'Get in under there,' he ordered Pinkie.

Pinkie pushed herself under the long clinging stems of the vine. The grey tom remained in the open, watching. 'Only just in time,' he whispered. 'Look!'

Pinkie peered between the stalks. She looked along the top of the wall. There was a bark, a scrabbling noise and then she saw a huge animal heave itself over the coping only metres away from where they had just been. It leapt down into the butcher's yard, growling, and, seeing the lamb bones, snatched them up and galloped back to the wall – all in a matter of seconds. Then it was up and over and into the park without spying Toby and almost before Pinkie had taken another breath.

'He's very fast,' said Toby. 'He has to be – the men would come after him with sticks. I've seen it happen.'

The sight of the great beast had made Pinkie forget the

liver. 'I'm not venturing here again,' she muttered. 'A few moments' delay and we'd have been lost.'

Toby was retrieving his sausages. The episode was over as far as he was concerned. 'That's why you need me,' he said quietly. 'I know all about this "food run". I know the signs to look out for. But if you won't come yourself, I can fetch for you.' He looked at her intently. 'As long as you promise,' he said, 'to stay by me. I mean always.'

Pinkie held his gaze. She knew what he referred to. He wanted her to become his mate and stay with him even if Sammy did return. What was she to do? It would certainly help to have regular supplies of meat brought for her and – eventually – the kittens. She didn't relish the prospect of exposing herself to the risk of colliding one day with the huge black dog. And it did seem as if Toby was offering himself as a sort of protector to her and her family. In Sammy's absence that was no bad thing. Perhaps he never would return. She wasn't even sure if he was still alive. She wavered. Toby waited for a reply.

'You put me in a quandary,' she murmured. 'You must know that Sammy has a prior claim on my loyalty. Something must have happened to him. And yet, he has always been keen for adventure – perhaps he has found something more exciting to do.'

Toby lost no time in playing on Pinkie's doubts. 'He's forgotten you, Pinkie,' he said categorically. 'You might as well forget him. Why waste a moment dwelling on the past? That cat has just left you in the lurch. How would he know if you've even survived until now? But you can depend on me.'

His words found their mark. Pinkie's disappointment with Sammy began to turn to resentment. 'You're right, I suppose,' she said finally. 'I don't know why I've kept him in my thoughts for so long.'

'Does that mean–?' Toby began hopefully.

'It means that I agree to your terms. As long as you see me and my young ones are fed and sheltered from danger, I'll stick with you. You have my word.'

'I ask no more,' said Toby, delighted. 'And you won't regret it.' He started to eat his sausages.

Pinkie finished the piece of liver. 'I used to drink from the park lake,' she told him. 'Is there anywhere nearer?'

Toby swallowed a mouthful. 'Oh, water's never a problem,' he said. 'The simple rule is to go where the birds go. A puddle, a dripping tap, a flat roof, a gutter – there's always something. We'll find water, never fear.' He pulled the remaining sausages under the thick strands of ivy, to return to in the future. 'Come on, Pinkie,' he said. 'I'll show you more of our territory.'

Pinkie didn't fail to catch the word 'our'. It told her clearly just how binding was her new commitment to Toby. She suffered some pangs of guilt for her inconstancy to the mate she had chosen in Quartermile Field. But now it was too late. 'Oh Sammy,' she whispered to herself, 'what have I done?'

Lizzie Reed soon discovered that the scraps of food she so patiently collected and deposited in the park for Pinkie were no longer sought by the little white cat. She found them untouched and, after a few days, she ceased to bring anything. She feared the worst for Pinkie whom she hadn't seen around for quite a while. And, thinking about Pinkie, Lizzie was naturally led to think of Sammy – the 'Puss' she had so conscientiously nursed back to health. Where was he now? She had no illusions about ever seeing him again. But she would have dearly loved to know just where he was and how he was surviving alone in an unknown part of the metropolis.

Sammy, of course, was not alone. Thanks to the houseboat owner, Elsie, he was being launched on a whole new career. The day after he had so rashly jumped on to the deck of the craft to exhibit his prowess as a hunter, he was taken by Elsie in a basket to her place of work. The woman had made quite sure he had no opportunity to escape and he had spent the previous night in the company of Smartie who had been told to 'guard him'.

Elsie's office was a ramshackle building south of the River Thames. Sammy was miles from his destination in the park and, even if he had been allowed the freedom to wander, he wouldn't have had an inkling of which direction to take. There was no canal to guide him now. But all that was immaterial. He was shut in the three-storey building where Elsie helped to run a small Direct Mail company. He had been set to patrol the rabbit-warren of corridors, corners and cubby-holes for marauding mice. To encourage him in his endeavours he was given nothing to eat in the belief that the hungrier he became, the keener he would be to seek out his prey. This new imprisonment was far worse than the monotony and boredom of life behind the walls of Lizzie Reed's flat. Sammy had never been so miserable.

The mice in Penstemon Buildings were old hands at avoiding predators. They had multiplied at the expense of a succession of cats and, indeed, human efforts at pest control. There was nothing they didn't know about the geography of the place, whether behind or in front of the ancient skirting-boards and wood panelling. They had the most elaborate system of tunnels and runs which wound up and down and around all three storeys. The offices were a paradise for these little creatures. They enjoyed free run of the poky rooms and their furniture, and their sharp teeth got to work on anything that could remotely come under the heading of edible. Into this mouse Utopia Sammy was introduced.

To his sensitive hunter's nose the smell of mice was overpowering. His sharp ears picked out the scratchings and the patterings of their tiny feet behind the panelling. Of course, during office hours, the mice mostly kept themselves out of sight. Sammy was set down without food in a disused corridor and told by Elsie in no uncertain terms to get on with his job. Sammy roamed up and down. There was no exit except a door which was kept shut. He was so bored he kept his nose pressed to the skirting board, first at one spot and then at another, listening to the squeaky voices of the mouse population and trying to catch a glimpse of them through cracks in the wall. This was his sole occupation on the first day. From time to time Elsie or another member of staff opened the door a fraction to see what he was up to. They thought his interest in the mice looked promising.

'You wait till tonight,' Elsie told her colleagues. 'He'll be so hungry he'll make mincemeat of them. Just let them dare to set foot outside their tunnels and he'll be on them. He's hot stuff, that cat.'

Some of the other employees were not too happy when it came to closing time and it appeared there was to be no food provided all night. Elsie plonked a bowl of water against a wall. 'That's all he'll need,' she declared. 'We'll see in the morning how he's done and if he's produced results we'll give him a reward. Believe me, it's the best way. What would be the sense in feeding him now? His incentive to hunt for himself would be gone. Remember the other cats.'

That night Sammy was to be allowed free run of all the offices and rooms. The mice inhabited the entire building and, once it grew dark and quiet, they could emerge just about anywhere. All doors were left ajar and propped open. Sammy was given words of encouragement and a stroke or two by the more kindly members of staff. Then he was left to his own devices as the lights were switched off.

As soon as he knew himself to be alone Sammy began to search for the food which he was sure would have been left for him. He had eaten very little during the last two days and he was very hungry. He explored room by room, passage by passage. He soon realized there was nothing. He didn't understand why he had been neglected in this way. His experience with Lizzie Reed made these humans' behaviour towards him all the more puzzling. He sought in vain for the smallest scrap of food.

During the night the mice, bold as ever, began to scurry about. Sammy heard them. He ran from room to room but, as soon as he entered a particular room, the mice that had been there dived back into their secret tunnels and then emerged somewhere else. Sammy chased their shrill squeaks in and out of the offices. They were too quick for him. They were past masters at evading predators. It was a game for the mice. They had a distinct advantage over Sammy in that they had so many tiny entrance and exit holes to the various parts of the building that even if he'd been there a year he could never have discovered them all.

Sammy changed his tactics. He stopped dashing from one place to another and chose one particular room, where there was a soft carpet to lie on. He was losing interest in hunting mice. He felt they had made him appear foolish and he needed to concentrate on getting himself out of this place. He recalled how he had escaped from Lizzie's flat and he wondered if he could employ the same trick here. The trouble was, there were so many doors here that he had no way of distinguishing which one was the way to the outside. So he couldn't decide where to station himself to wait for the office workers to return to the building. There was no doubt they would come back, he told himself, endeavouring to keep up his courage.

While Sammy lay unhappily on the carpet, the mice chatted amongst themselves about this new predator brought in to disrupt their lives. From past experience they were scornful of the cat's abilities.

'Another one to go the same way as his predecessors,' they said.

'Here today, gone tomorrow,' they said.

'He's got about as much chance of scattering us as a dog with three legs,' scoffed one older mouse.

'Have they left any food for him?' asked a relative.

'Let's go and look. They usually do.'

Sammy's eyes had remained open. He looked perfectly harmless as he lolled on the floor with his back resting against the leg of a desk. The mice were convinced he had given up any pretence of a chase and eventually some of them, in their quest for the cat's food supply, ventured into the office where Sammy lay. Sammy heard their skinny little feet and their tinny little voices approaching. These sounds were so familiar he found himself trying to recall why. Then he remembered his days as a kitten in Mrs Lambert's garden shed when he had made friends with a young mouse called Tiptoe. Now these sounds, identical to Tiptoe's, brought those days back to him. Sammy was aware of the irony of his present position. Times had changed indeed. He was no kitten, fed by human hand and ready to befriend a mouse. How dare these puny creatures here take him for granted, as if he were of no account? He didn't give up so easily and they were going to find they had made a mistake. He tensed. His every sense was alert, strained to the utmost to utilize every chance and advantage. Two mice scurried across the floor, pausing to raise themselves on their hind feet as they sniffed, searching for odours of cat food. Sammy was perfectly still, rigid as stone, yet as taut as a drawn bow. The mice strayed too close. Their contempt or arrogance –

whatever it was – was their undoing. Sammy sprang. The mice scuttled for their escape route. They were astonishingly quick. One of the dived into the hole behind the skirting board from which they had emerged. The other tumbled after him but Sammy fastened on to his tail. The mouse was yanked free from the wall and Sammy had his first taste of live prey for many a week.

The young tabby was mightily heartened. He didn't dash about now, alerting every mouse to his presence – he stalked them. He used his wits and intelligence and was no longer content to remain on one floor. He crept upstairs on noiseless feet, his tawny body low-slung, his whiskers brushing the wall. Three more mice were seized before the night was out. As the late winter dawn stole over the city, their companions hid themselves away and held counsel. Sammy the hunter was not to be despised.

—9—

Cat and mouse

The mice in Penstemon Buildings were an old-established colony and generations of them had lived – and mostly thrived – there. The appearance of Sammy on the scene gave them a lot to think about. For the first time in ages they discovered themselves to be in very real danger and they didn't like it one bit. They chattered incessantly about what they must do, how they should get rid of the problem, but no one came up with a definite plan. It was apparent that they needed to be more cautious than ever before but, other than that – well, what else was there to do?

In the morning Elsie arrived and promptly toured the offices, room by room, looking for signs that Sammy had done his duty. She ignored the cat, even though he followed her round, eager for a show of friendliness after his long period of solitude. The woman found the remains of four mouse carcasses. Elsie was triumphant. She removed the debris and at last stooped to give Sammy an acknowledging pat.

'You've made a good start,' Elsie crowed, 'and you shall be rewarded. But not with too much – you've got a long way to go and I don't want you to lose interest.'

She was true to her word. She put a small quantity of cat food in a saucer and put it in the disused corridor where

Sammy had been installed to make his first patrol. The poor cat, whose stomach had had almost nothing in it for two days, leapt upon the food and wolfed it down. Then he began to look around for more. He had become used to the generous portions Lizzie had given him and Elsie's paltry offering was nowhere near enough.

Elsie watched him, nodding her head as she did so. 'Yes, you could eat a bigger plateful, no doubt,' she said to Sammy. 'But that's not my policy. We want this place rid of mice. And tonight we'll let you into the warehouse. You'll have a field day. I'll bet you won't feel hungry tomorrow and then you won't need *any* of this tinned stuff.'

Work began and Sammy was permitted to wander about, seeking in vain for that other plate of food he was convinced must have been hidden somewhere else. He looked so puzzled and unsettled that one of Elsie's colleagues took pity on him and gave him some milk in the afternoon.

'No good spoiling him, Viv,' Elsie admonished her. 'He's here for a purpose.'

'It's only a drop of milk,' Viv protested. 'And, poor creature, he looks so – so wild.'

'He *is* wild. I told you how I came by him. He's a stray; turned up out of the blue. How else could I have brought him here? I didn't kidnap him!'

'Even if he is a stray I can't help feeling sorry for him,' Viv insisted. 'He doesn't look at all happy.'

'He's not here to be happy. No good making him comfortable, is it? The wretched little mice are too comfortable here, that's the whole trouble.'

They were less comfortable than they had been, though, thanks to Sammy. Moreover, this cat didn't seem to have brought with him the benefit of the bowls of food with which the mice had always been pleased to complement their diet. Try as they would, they could find no remnants of cat food anywhere.

The second night Sammy was given access to the warehouse. Amongst the packing materials, the paper, the card, the pallets, and the parcels, the mice of Penstemon Buildings were more active than anywhere else. It was incredible what they considered edible. They raided, and nibbled at everything. The tiniest scrap of food left by one of the packers – crumbs of biscuit or sandwiches or chocolate – were seized. But the paper itself was chewed, too, torn into shreds and either used for bedding or eaten. Until Sammy came.

He chased them along the counter, over the floor, on top of the piles of paper, and in and out of packages and boxes. And he caught them. He caught many of them. The others deserted the warehouse. Defeat and a mass exodus stared them in the face.

Behind the walls, under the floorboards, they raged at the cat who was more than their match.

'What now?' they asked. 'He'll drive us out. From our home – our hereditary home. There have always been Penstemon Mice. And, where would we go?'

One elder mouse tried to calm the uproar. 'Listen,' he said, 'it won't come to the worst. We won't quit. We must come to an arrangement.'

'What arrangement?' cried the others.

'An agreement,' said the old mouse, 'with the tabby cat. He doesn't get fed and –'

'That's why he eats us!' piped up a terrified youngster before he could finish.

'Be quiet a moment,' said the old mouse whose name was Nip. 'Listen to me. The cat is starved deliberately so that he hunts all the time. He can't escape from here. The humans shut him in, don't they? But supposing we tell him of our escape route? If he's being held here against his will – and I think he is – he'll jump at our offer. Then, in return for our secret, he must hunt us no more!'

'That's brilliant!' the mice cried. They were at their wits' end. But some of them grumbled beneath their breath, doubting it would be so simple.

One of the doubters waited for the hubbub to die down. Then he said cynically, 'I'm sure we'll all rush to be the volunteer to talk to the cat.'

There was total silence. Evidently none of them had thought of that. They began to look towards Nip, mumbling amongst themselves that, as he had made the suggestion, why shouldn't he be the one to do the talking? Nip saw the mass of faces turned towards him, each one with whiskers twitching nervously.

'All right,' he said. 'I'll speak to him. But from a safe place. And, while I'm doing it, the rest of you had better get to work on enlarging our escape passage.'

Under the floorboards, scores of mice sharpened their incisors and then the rasping of hundreds of rodent teeth could be heard as they chiselled through rotten wood and other obstructions to the outside wall leading on to the street. Here where a few loose bricks gave access to the open air an ancient mouse exit had been used in times of necessity by countless animals. Now, however, the loose bricks needed to be removed altogether to enable the tabby cat to make his departure. The mice questioned whether this difficult task should be begun before they knew if Sammy had accepted the bargain. They decided they should hold back until Nip reported back to them. For the present they needed this bolt-hole to be cat-proof in case they themselves turned out to be the ones that would have to leave. . . .

Nip ran under the floorboards, stopping now and then at a mouse spy-hole to check how close he was getting to the cat. Sammy was lying by some piles of envelopes, resting after his exertions. Nip wanted to get as near as he could without in any way endangering himself. At last, at a distance of about the length of a cat's tail he put his mouth to the spy-hole and, squeaking at the top of his voice, called to the cat.

Sammy instantly jumped up and bounded to the hole. His huge eyes peered through and Nip, terrified, fell back and tumbled over himself in his alarm. But he summoned up all his courage and tried again.

'Cat, do you hear me? I've a pro-prop-proposition to make,' he stammered.

Sammy glared silently. He could see nothing in the darkness. However, Nip's squeal, so reminiscent of Tiptoe's, was perfectly audible. He waited.

'Do you want to get out of here?' came the mouse voice.

'What if I do?' Sammy hissed down the hole. He was giving nothing away yet.

Nip, his fur billowing in the hot cat breath, retreated a centimetre or two. He didn't wish to be deafened. 'We can help you,' he offered. 'There is a way out.'

Now Sammy was interested. Pinkie, the park, freedom – things he had almost accepted as lost for ever – suddenly beckoned to him again. 'What's your proposition?' he asked.

'That we come to an agreement,' said Nip. 'You give us your word to cease hunting and we – we mice – get you out.'

'Keep talking,' said Sammy. 'Where is this way out?'

'Under the floor; we'll show you where. But first, your promise.'

'Why should I promise first?' Sammy asked suspiciously. 'How do I know you won't lead me up a blind alley?'

'There's no blind alley,' Nip answered impatiently.

'Listen. Can't you hear that noise?' He fell silent. The regular scraping and rasping of mice teeth was easily detectable.

'Yes, I hear it,' Sammy admitted. 'What of it?'

'The mice are constructing a passage for you to the outside,' Nip explained. 'Our mouse runs would other-wise be too small for you. Could there be any better proof that you can trust us to keep our side of the bargain?'

Sammy understood the mice really did mean business. 'All right then,' he said. 'I agree not to hunt you any more so long as you conduct me out of this building. But I want something else from you too.'

'What else? Isn't that enough?' Nip squeaked angrily.

'No, it isn't enough,' Sammy returned. 'Because I need you to give me directions. I don't know where I've been brought; I don't know this building, and I want to get back to the area I know. How can I do that, even if you do get me into the open again? I'd be lost before I could start.'

'That's not our problem,' Nip snapped. '*We* didn't bring you here and we don't know where you come from. This request is absurd and unreasonable.'

'Then it's no deal,' Sammy remarked coolly. 'I may as well stay here.' He raised himself and walked away from the hole with an obstinate expression. Stupid mice, they'll soon come to their senses, he thought.

Nip was stunned. He had been so sure he had found the perfect solution to the colony's safety. This tabby cat was a ridiculous creature. How dare he make his own demands? The old mouse was furious. Let him remain a prisoner then! But Nip soon realized this would also be the worst possible scenario for the mice. And they would blame him. He crept away from the hole, looking very distressed.

The other mice soon began to gather round Nip, expecting to hear good news. But when they saw his face they became very anxious. A chorus of questions delivered in every register of squeak and squeal resounded in the subterranean mouse galleries. Up above, Sammy heard this new noise which had replaced the sound of gnawing. Nip tried to explain what had gone wrong but it was impossible to make himself heard. At last the voices subsided. Nip related Sammy's demand in a tone of defeat. Immediately a fresh vocal storm broke over him, this time of protests and accusations. The old mouse seemed to shrink into himself beneath this torrent of indignation.

'What could I do?' he asked feebly. 'How could I direct the cat anywhere? *I* don't know where it came from!'

'Didn't you ask? Didn't you ask?' the mice clamoured in disbelief.

'N-no, I didn't,' Nip confessed humbly.

'This is incredible,' said another senior mouse. 'You had a chance to rid us of this menace and you – you just played right into the cat's paws – I should say jaws. The animal doesn't want to leave, it's too happy decimating our population!'

'That's not true!' Nip cried. 'The animal admitted it wanted to get away from here. I did my best. I faced the enemy and spoke up. I didn't notice *you* leaping to volunteer.'

'Either way, the chance was lost,' the other elderly mouse mumbled.

The mice drifted away in little knots, chattering to each other about what the outcome would be. They all foresaw another night of slaughter.

—10—

Trust and mistrust

But first, for mice and cat alike, there were the daylight hours to get through. Elsie arrived for work, bringing her dog Smartie with her. A quick count of the dead mice in the warehouse, very few of which Sammy had attempted to eat, told Elsie that her campaign against the mice was proving successful. Sammy was rewarded with nothing more than a saucer of milk. After demolishing it he didn't bother this time to look for more. He knew better. Smartie came up to him, his tail wagging briskly. To his surprise, Sammy spat at him!

'Why are you like this?' Smartie asked, puzzled. 'I thought you'd be pleased to see me.'

'Pleased to see *you*?' Sammy growled. 'You've been no friend to me. You tricked me on to your floating home so that your cruel mistress could trap me. Look at this place! What sort of life for a cat is this, shut up day and night?'

'But you're a hunter,' Smartie said, genuinely perplexed. 'I thought you –'

'Never mind what you thought,' Sammy snapped. 'There's more to a cat's life than catching mice. When you first saw me I was at liberty to go where I chose, not confined to a few dark and gloomy passages. That's what you've condemned me to with your treachery!'

Smartie backed away, truly shaken by the ferocity of the

cat's words. He was almost convinced that Sammy meant to attack him.

'I say, this has all been a misunderstanding,' he muttered awkwardly. 'I never suspected – I mean, look here, once you've rid this place of the mice there will be no reason for you to remain.'

'Rid this place!' Sammy bellowed. 'Have you any conception of the number of mice in this building? There are *hundreds*. I've heard them, gibbering and scratching. Am I to spend the rest of my life here?'

'I – well, I don't know. I'm sure my mistress would welcome you back to our boat on the canal, even if you couldn't quite – er – deal with every last mouse. You've made a big difference already, judging by the –'

Sammy wasn't listening. 'Canal?' he repeated. 'Canal? Is that the name of the long water?'

'L-long water?' Smartie gasped.

'Where you tricked me,' Sammy reminded him.

'I didn't, honestly -- but, yes, that's what it's called.'

'Good. You've been of some use,' Sammy growled. 'Now get away from me. You and your fat mistress make a good pair. Heartless, both of you. I would rather stay here than come and live with you two. I'd starve on that boat, as you call it. Have you seen how little she feeds me?'

Smartie felt there was no purpose in pursuing the conversation any further. More cowed by the tabby cat's fierceness than he cared to admit, he was only too glad to disappear and rejoin Elsie. Sammy was left to nurse his sense of grievance and to think about how he could rectify his mistake in rejecting the old mouse's offer.

That night Sammy set himself to force the issue. An even greater reduction in the colony's numbers this third night, Sammy calculated, must surely persuade the mice to re-open negotiations with him and, in so doing, almost certainly concede the extra terms he was demanding. But, in fact, the reverse of what he was planning occurred. He didn't catch a single mouse. He didn't see a single mouse. He heard them of course. Whispering and prattling in their underground network. But not one mouse dared to show itself. The colony was terrified. The mice had met their match and were keeping on the safe side of the walls and floorboards.

'We can't live like this,' they told each other.

'We can't huddle in a mass without food,' they complained.

'We need to fetch bedding,' the pregnant females protested. 'Something will have to be done.'

'Nip must talk to the hunter again,' they all decided. 'He has the cat's ear. Let him tell the animal we're prepared to do whatever it wants. We *must* make it go.'

At first Nip refused to put himself in the front line again. 'It's someone else's turn to play this game,' he grumbled. 'Small thanks I got for my efforts.'

But now the mice interrupted each other to lavish praise upon him for his bravery, his coolness, his diplomacy; they hadn't appreciated before, in their initial disappointment just what he had achieved. In the end Nip relented and, urged on by the others, pattered back to his spy-hole.

Sammy was in the warehouse, somewhat surprised that so far no mice had appeared, but readier than ever to pounce on the first one that did so. Nip watched him prowling for some moments. The tabby looked every inch the hunter and the old mouse was greatly comforted by the knowledge that not one member of the colony was contemplating breaking cover. In his rather quavery voice Nip began to call.

'Cat! Tabby Cat, we have to talk. Can you hear me?'

Sammy heard well enough. He approached the hole. 'Changed your mind, have you?' he crowed.

Nip saw no reason to hedge. 'Yes, we have,' he confessed. 'We want you to leave and we'll do our best to put you on the right track. Where do you wish to go?'

'To the canal,' Sammy replied promptly.

'The – what?'

'The canal, the canal! Don't be smart with me. I have to return to the long piece of water that's called the canal.'

'Ah, now I understand,' Nip said with some relief. He had never heard the word 'canal' but he knew all about the 'long piece of water' and assumed that Sammy was talking about the river which was very close. 'Yes, we can help you there. If that's your destination, then there's nothing simpler.'

Sammy began to feel optimistic. 'Well then?' he urged.

'Well, you won't have a very long journey,' Nip told him.

'Yes, but the route, the route,' Sammy prompted impatiently.

'All in good time,' said the mouse. 'First you have to renew your promise not to attack any of us.'

'Oh, you have it, you have it,' Sammy answered with exasperation. 'Must we discuss this all night?'

'No. We're as eager as you are for an end to this,' Nip assured him. 'I'll go at once and give instructions for your exit to be completed.'

Sammy resumed his prowling around the warehouse. However, this time he was prowling to use up the minutes rather than as a hunter. The rasping of incisor teeth was soon once more to be heard.

The mice worked with a will and the task of enlarging their passage to the outside wall was soon accomplished. There now remained only the actual exit through the wall to be excavated, as well as making an entry point wide enough through the floor for Sammy to get into the tunnel. The latter presented no problem, since the mice were dealing merely with wooden floor-boards. But, try as they did with as many helpers as could be mustered at the wall, the mice just hadn't sufficient strength to make any impression on brick. Work on Sammy's entrance hole was stopped at once. The mice couldn't risk allowing the tabby into their underground domain before his exit through the building wall was complete. The slaughter he had caused before would be as nothing to the mayhem he could unleash once inside their tunnels. The mice gathered around Nip, looking at each other in consternation.

'We can't move the brick,' they chanted. 'It's too heavy. It won't budge.'

'But the bricks are loose, are they not?' Nip queried anxiously.

'Loose, but not loose enough for mice,' came the reply. 'What do we do now, Nip? The cat will be furious if it's thwarted.'

'Wait, let me think.'

The mice milled around, all in a twitter. At last Nip spoke.

'There's only one solution,' he said gravely, 'and it's one that alarms me considerably. We don't know how far we can trust the cat and we *will* need to put a great deal of trust in him. Now, before you all create an uproar about what I'm going to say, let me tell you I'm only making such a suggestion because the alternative would be even worse.'

The mice were agog. Many of them felt their fate was in the balance.

'We need strength,' Nip continued amid total silence, 'far greater than mice-strength to dislodge those bricks. Now, the tabby cat, as we know to our cost, is a strong animal.' He paused, waiting for his words to penetrate. 'Supposing he were to use his greater strength on the bricks?'

One old mouse, who had disputed with Nip before, asked drily, 'And where will we all be whilst the cat is at the end of our tunnel tugging at the bricks?'

'We'd have to keep out of his way as best we could,' Nip replied quietly.

The uproar he had expected now occurred. 'Impossible!' the mice cried. 'We couldn't hide ourselves, not the entire colony. If the cat couldn't move the bricks there'd be a massacre. He'd be right in amongst us. There'd be no escape.'

When Nip could make himself heard again he said, 'Then the only alternative is to remain as we are, each of us running the gauntlet of his attacks night after night.'

The colony was quick to appreciate that this was unthinkable. It might lead eventually to the extinction of the entire population. They began to see that the only way to proceed was Nip's way.

'We do have one thing in our favour to ensure he keeps his side of the bargain,' the old mouse said encouragingly. 'He wants to return to the river. He depends on us to tell him how to reach it. And we won't do that until he's outside the wall.'

'And if he's not strong enough to move the loose bricks?' a voice piped up.

'Then we're all lost, whatever happens,' Nip replied fatalistically. 'But why think of the worst? Let's keep our hopes up.'

The others accepted they had no option.

'Finish off the entry hole,' Nip told them. 'I'll go and speak to the cat and tell him what he has to do.'

Sammy hadn't ceased to pace for a moment. He ran to the mouse hole at the first sound of Nip's squeaking. He listened attentively.

'You have my word, my hunting days are over here,' he told Nip soberly. He was eager only for escape. 'I long for

nothing more than to be on the other side of the wall.' He
even agreed to wait for the vital directions to the waterside
until he had gained the open air. Like the mice, Sammy
realized there was no viable alternative to the plan.

'Show me where I must enter,' he bade Nip.

Minutes later, after the mouse colony had had time to
take what precautions it could, Sammy left the warehouse
through a jagged hole in the floor which the mice had
constructed for him. He found himself in a tunnel only just
wide and deep enough to accommodate his body. His
back scraped the floorboards above, his sides brushed
unseen obstacles. He scrambled along in a half-crouch
while his belly bumped the ground. It was easy to direct
himself to the wall. The mouse-sized hole that already
existed between the bricks let in enough light to guide
him. He reached the exit and peered through the gap.
Sure enough, he glimpsed the street outside. The mice,
who had secreted themselves at the farthest point of their
labyrinths, waited with bated breath. They heard the
scrape of brick against brick as Sammy tugged with his
paws to enlarge the hole. The tabby was filled with
excitement. The fresh air of freedom was so close he could
smell it. Any satisfaction he had felt honing his hunting
techniques in this gloomy building was easily eclipsed by
such a tantalising promise of liberty. He was absolutely
determined he would get through this barrier. And, at
last, the loose bricks shifted. Sammy's head popped
through the widened gap. Then, elongating his body in a
wonderfully elastic feline movement, he slipped through
to the street.

Odours, fragrances – fresh clean smells of the night air –
wafted to his nostrils. Sammy breathed deeply and
gratefully. For the third time he had escaped from a
prison. He turned and looked back through the hole in the
wall. Pride and a little naiveté had led to his imprisonment

this last time. Never, never would he trust another human.

He had, however, trusted the mice he had so recently been hunting and they had trusted him. He called back to them. 'I'm free and you're safe. Come and give me my directions.'

It was Nip, of course, who came running first. Some of the other mice followed him at a distance, suspicious to the end. Nip looked at the new hole and marvelled. He could hardly believe that a cat could have so shaped his body as to have got through such a narrow gap. But there was Sammy on the other side. In a flash Nip realized that if the tabby had got through once, he could get back again. The colony wasn't safe quite yet. . . .

'I'm going to give you the best help I can,' Nip told the tabby cautiously, 'but you'll understand I have to cover every loophole. I must request that you first close up the gap in the bricks, just in case another hunter comes snooping.'

Sammy wasn't fooled for a moment. He knew the mouse was, in reality, thinking of him. He grinned a cat grin and, without a word, leant his strong shoulder against the loosened brickwork. The gap closed in a tricc. Nip squeaked his delight.

'Now, Mouse,' said Sammy.

'Now, Cat. Look towards the end of the street. Take that direction. Eventually you will smell fish. When the smell is at its strongest, look up. You'll see a low wall – low for you, at any rate. Mice would need to climb that wall; *you* can jump it. You will then be out of the street and in a dark alley narrow for men. There is a gutter, usually full of good mouse food. Follow the gutter, it runs downhill. At the end of the gutter you will see and hear and smell the river. It is not a long journey for a cat, but beware of the rats.'

'The river? The river?' Sammy repeated.

'Yes, the long water.'

'Ah.'

'I leave you,' said Nip, and scuttled away.

Sammy cast a last glance at Penstemon Buildings and, with the mouse's instructions still ringing in his head, headed for the end of the street.

—11—

The heart of London

The night was quiet as Sammy walked along Peascod Street, sniffing vigorously for that first whiff of fish. He paused once or twice, not quite sure whether he had located it or not. After a hundred metres or so the aroma was unmistakable. It was fried fish he could smell from the fish and chip shop at the end of the street. Sammy looked up.

' "A low wall",' he quoted. And there it was – barely a wall at all, but he supposed to a mouse it would appear to be one. He vaulted over it and was at once plunged into greater darkness as he entered the alley between two buildings. It was a collection area for dustbins and rubbish bags. Litter and garbage lay underfoot. Sammy wrinkled his nose distastefully. Food for mice and rats it may be, but these sour rotting smells were of no attraction to him. A drainage gutter ran down the centre of the alley. Sammy followed it along. It began to dip downward. His anticipation grew. At any moment he expected to see the canal again. He was buoyant. The injury no longer troubled him in the slightest; and he was on his way back to Pinkie.

And then he saw the water. He began to run. He couldn't believe his eyes. This vast, wide, moving expanse lit by a mass of reflected light was no canal. He jumped on to a parapet of the river wall and watched. It flowed endlessly past like a monstrous living thing, surging forward on its own secret purpose. This watercourse was greater even than the river he had discovered in the neighbourhood of his old home in Quartermile Field. Sammy was overawed; then his thoughts turned to the Penstemon mice and he was angry. They had fooled him and now he was lost. How could he ever find Pinkie again? He jumped to the ground and started to run back up the alley. He'd show those mice the consequences of not keeping their side of the bargain!

He thought he saw movement ahead. He stopped. He recalled the warning about rats. He crept forward. 'What are rats to me?' he scoffed. 'I've caught and killed rats before. They may frighten mice but –' Suddenly he was surrounded and almost bowled over by what seemed like a tide of moving bodies. A horde of brown rats, out scavenging for whatever they could find, had rushed towards him. Sammy leapt clear and landed on top of a pile of rubbish bags. It was these bags that had been the rats' target. They gathered around them, systematically ripping out the contents with their sharp teeth and claws. Sammy teetered as the pile began to collapse.

'Get out of our way!' some of the rats cried viciously. They knew they were in no danger of attack from a cat while they so outnumbered him.

Sammy could see that anything would be fair game to this horde. They looked murderous. All the time, more were arriving to swell the numbers. They were coming from underneath the road surface, squeezing between the gratings and squealing to each other in their determination to get to the food source before their fellows. Sammy poised himself for a great jump, aiming to land clear of this brown sea of scavengers.

He jumped and landed in their midst but the rats,

intent on their goal, rushed past him. Sammy took to his feet and fled blindly back up the alley. He didn't stop until he had regained Peascod Street. Outside the fish and chip shop a skinny black and white cat was eating something off the pavement. Sammy perked up. It was a long time since he had seen one of his own kind and this cat, moreover, was a female. He forgot all about the rats as he approached her, intending to be friendly.

The female saw Sammy and mistook his intention. She snatched up the food – a discarded fried fishtail – and began to run.

'Wait! Wait!' Sammy called. 'I want to talk to you.'

The other cat paused and looked back, her eyes full of alarm. She was ready to bolt in a second.

'I'm not after your food,' Sammy assured her, although he was in fact extremely hungry. 'I need your help.'

The black and white cat gulped down the morsel of food. 'Help. From me?' she asked cynically. 'How on earth should I be able to help anyone?' She had a rough voice.

'Because you must know this area,' said Sammy, 'and I want to know if you've ever heard of the canal?'

'Don't know what you're talking about.'

Sammy tried to explain, comparing it with what he had just seen.

'Nothing like that around here. There's only the river.'

'Is that where I've just been?'

'Sounds like it. Look, what is all this?'

'I'm trying to find my home,' Sammy told her. He stopped himself from mentioning Pinkie; he didn't know why. 'I'm lost, you see.' He described how he had been captured by Elsie.

The female cat was inclined to be sympathetic. 'Perhaps what you're looking for is on the other side of the river.'

'The other side? Well then, I'm beaten,' Sammy replied morosely. 'No animal could swim across that great –'

'Don't be stupid!' the female cat said sharply. 'There are bridges. You can walk over.'

'Where? Where? Oh tell me, please.'

'Look, I've enough to do finding sufficient to eat without guiding strange cats around the place.'

'Of course. I didn't mean to . . . Hey! I know what.' Sammy brightened. 'I'm a good hunter. I'll find us both food; I'm pretty near starving myself. When we've eaten, maybe you could show me this bridge?'

The female cat calculated. 'There's precious little except rats to hunt around here,' she remarked dourly. But she rather liked the idea of teaming up with a good hunter. She could never get enough to eat.

'Wait here,' Sammy said and, on an impulse, turned and entered the dark alley again.

Rats, their jaws crammed with stinking provisions, were scattering, scurrying for the drain-holes through which they returned to the sanctuary of the sewer system. Some were still bickering, fighting for a greater share of the garbage. Sammy took one of these unawares and despatched the animal quickly. The other rats were oblivious. Sammy carried the rat carefully back to the female cat. He had no taste for the thing himself.

'Here you are,' he said. 'It's the best I can do at the moment.'

'Thanks,' she said in her rough voice. 'What do I call you?'

'Sammy. And you?'

'Phoebe.' She fell on the rat, tearing at it, devouring it without compunction. Sammy felt chastened. What was *his* hunger compared to this? He returned for another kill.

A little later Sammy and Phoebe sat looking at the skin and bone of two rat carcasses.

'Why didn't you eat some if you're hungry?' she enquired.

'Oh, I – er – I'm just eager to get to that bridge,' Sammy waffled.

Phoebe licked her chops. 'I'm almost persuaded to come with you,' she said pensively. 'You are a good hunter.'

Sammy was pleased by her remark. He had been solitary for a long time. But what about Pinkie? It could be awkward. 'It's for you to decide,' he replied, avoiding direct encouragement.

'Follow me,' said the black and white cat. 'We need to cross the bridge in darkness.' She took the direction of Penstemon Buildings. Evidently the way to the bridge was not the same as the way to the river.

She trotted along briskly. Sammy kept by her side. They maintained silence, passing Penstemon Buildings and arriving at the opposite end of Peascod Street. Now Phoebe's knowledge of the streets and lanes came into its own. She headed for the bridge by the safest route. They crossed some public gardens and came to a broad riverside walk, at the end of which was a long flight of steps. Phoebe led Sammy up these to the bridge. To Sammy it seemed like a broad avenue. There were pavements on either side.

'We're crossing the river,' Phoebe informed him as she ran on, eager to reach a less exposed spot. There were only a few people and vehicles about. Daylight was beginning to appear. Sammy was in the very heart of London, on Westminster Bridge.

A few minutes later Phoebe said, 'Now I no longer know where we are.' They had reached the north side of the river. She looked at Sammy uncertainly. 'This is all new territory to me,' she said. 'I ought to get back to what I know.'

'I'm grateful to you,' Sammy said. 'Maybe we'll meet again?'

'That's unlikely,' Phoebe countered. 'You won't be coming back to my part of the city.'

'No. Well, I'm sorry we didn't get to know each other better.' There was something about this cat, rough and skinny as she was, that Sammy liked. And she had been of great help.

'I'm sorry too,' said Phoebe. They looked at each other a moment longer. 'You'd better move to a quieter spot,' she advised, 'before the humans really get going.'

Sammy looked around. Across the other side of the bridge was the Houses of Parliament, a huge edifice which he wanted to avoid. He made a right turn from the bridge, steering clear of the alarmingly complex crossroads and walked along the pavement on the river side of the Victoria Embankment. Opposite him was a patch of greenery which reminded him of the park and which seemed an oasis of tranquillity away from the network of roads. As soon as he thought it was safe, he didn't hesitate. He sprinted across to it and found himself in a sort of garden. For some reason he turned. To his surprise there was Phoebe, still sitting where he had left her. She had been watching his progress and apparently was still considering whether she should join him.

Sammy was not in a position to wait. He wanted to get under cover and, before this, to see to his empty stomach. The garden was just a patch of green in front of another large building. Sammy had seen sufficient buildings now to be careless of them. He was much more interested in a blackbird that was tugging at a worm in the lawn. It was very absorbed by its task. But it never did get the worm. Sammy pounced, and it was the cat that enjoyed a breakfast, not the bird.

The tabby glanced about for a place to hide. He needed

to be well and truly away from the grasp of human hands. He was not going to be tilted off course a third time by human intervention. But what course? How was he to find the canal now?

'Some creature must know of the canal or the park,' he told himself optimistically. He could find nowhere suitable for shelter nearby so he ran along, close to the bare plane trees of the embankment, searching all the while for a retreat. Every now and then he turned his head to see if Phoebe might, after all, have come after him. He was sure she wouldn't have needed a lot of persuasion to do so. But he didn't see her and, before long, he had found what he wanted and settled himself under an evergreen shrub in the Victoria Embankment Gardens. He was a little less hungry, and very tired. It had been an eventful few hours. He made himself comfortable and was soon enjoying a refreshing doze.

Well on in the morning Sammy's nap was interrupted by a squirrel which was busying itself unearthing buried nuts. The scratching of the animal's claws on the soil all around where Sammy had chosen to sleep disturbed him. The cat yawned and watched the quick movements of the squirrel. The little creature seemed not in the least perturbed by the presence of an animal larger than itself.

'Difficult finding food?' the cat enquired lazily.

'Always is in the winter months, especially when you can't remember exactly where you hid your winter provisions,' the squirrel answered without halting its digging for one moment. It found an acorn and, after examining it, sat back on its hind legs to eat.

'You seem quite at home here,' Sammy remarked. 'You don't take any precautions.'

'Precautions? What kind of precautions?' the squirrel asked between nibbles.

'Well, you wandered very close to me. Supposing I'd wanted to spring at you?'

'Then I'd have run,' said the squirrel. 'But you were asleep, and at times like this one has to grab one's chance when it comes. Food is scarce and the weather's about to get worse.'

'Do you think so?'

'I know it. I've lived long enough to be able to read the signs. So I'm filling up while I can because soon I'll be confined to my drey.'

'Is that your home?'

'Yes, it's over there in that tall tree.'

'How I wish my home was so close,' Sammy sighed. 'I don't even know how to find it again.'

'You don't know how to find your own home?'

'No. I was whisked away from it by a young human who wanted me to live with her like a pet. But I'm no pet!' Sammy flexed his muscles as he stretched.

'I can see that,' remarked the squirrel as it dug out another acorn. 'Where's *your* home then?'

'In the park – um – near the canal,' Sammy recited hopefully.

'Park? You're not too far from that,' he was told. The canal reference was ignored.

'Not too far? Oh, can you help me find it?' Sammy cried.

'I can't, I've never been there,' said the other animal. 'But I'll tell you what you can do. Go and ask the Trafalgar Square pigeons. They're real Londoners. They fly all over, and they're bound to know where the park is.'

'Pigeons?' Sammy muttered to himself. 'I hunt pigeons!' Then, aloud, 'Where is this place – the square you mentioned?'

The squirrel finished eating the acorn. 'Look,' he said, 'I don't go there myself. I don't like places without plenty of trees. The best thing for you to do is to wait here. It's a

fine day. There will be humans coming to eat here in a
while. They sit on those long wooden benches. They
always come at the same time, bringing their food with
them. The pigeons know this and they time their arrival
accordingly. The humans toss them titbits. They might
toss you some, too, if you hang around and look hungry.
And you *do* look hungry.'

'Yes, yes, I am,' Sammy admitted. 'But what about the
pigeons? You said "wait for the pigeons".'

'Oh yes. Well, some of them fly in from the square. So
they could point you towards it. Who knows, they may
even have visited your park. They cover great distances.
So you may get all the assistance you need. Otherwise go
to the Square and ask around. You're sure to get the
information eventually. Nothing pigeons like so much as
showing off their knowledge of the city.'

'Even to a cat?'

'Ah, well that could be a problem. My advice is: don't
be too cat-like.'

'Easier said than done. But thanks. I feel much more
hopeful.'

'Best of luck. And I hope you manage to get under cover
before the weather bites.'

Sammy was almost light-hearted as he waited for the
office picnickers to appear at their appointed hour. The
squirrel had vanished long before the first human seated
himself and began to unwrap his sandwiches. But the
animal's prediction was accurate enough. No sooner had
the first crumbs of bread fallen to the ground than pigeons
winged their way down to the gardens with practised
alacrity. In no time there were thirty or more of them
competing for each fragment of food. And in these pigeons
from the heart of London lay Sammy's best hope of
returning to Pinkie's side.

—12—

Toby turns

While Sammy was struggling to get back to her, Pinkie, in his absence, was forging closer links with the grey male cat Toby. The two of them had regular supplies of meat which they usually ate together amicably. She had come to rely on him more and more, now that the kittens were showing signs of interest in their surroundings. Toby played his part in ensuring that none of the little ones strayed too far. He knew all the likely dangers and alarms of the district and protected them from any mishap. And he tried to find suitable titbits for them when they began to eat solid food.

The kittens looked upon Toby as part of the family. They were, as yet, too young to learn about the difference between a father and a friend. Pinkie knew that the situation would one day have to be explained to them but for the moment she was content to leave things as they were. From time to time she still returned to the park in the forlorn hope of seeing Sammy reappear. She would patrol the length of the lake, always at night, occasionally calling to him. Then she would visit the old lair to leave her smell on the bamboo shrubbery before making her way back to the kittens and to Toby. She didn't really expect to see Sammy again. But for the sake of Fern, Moss and little Sammy, who had never known their father, she continued her sporadic searches.

On such occasions she always came back looking glum. Toby knew only too well where she had been and why, but he never passed comment. He would sometimes begin playing with one of the kittens, each of whom was always ready for a romp, as if underlining the fact that, as far as the youngsters were concerned, they didn't actually need their real father. They were perfectly happy as they were.

'Don't be too rough with them,' Pinkie would tell the tom. 'You don't know your own strength.'

'Of course I do,' he'd reply. 'They'll come to no harm with me, you should know that.'

Pinkie had to admit, 'Yes, you've been good to them – and to me.'

'I've never been so content with my lot,' Toby would say.

Pinkie would look at him with the beginnings of an affection and then, almost as if struck by a feeling of guilt, would turn away again hastily and gaze in the direction of the park with a wistful expression.

They were sitting on the park wall one night when Toby said bluntly to Pinkie, 'What would you do if Sammy came back?'

Pinkie didn't answer at once. She didn't know how to reply. An owl flitted through the park's open spaces above them. Eventually she said, 'It's really more a question of what Sammy would do. Isn't it?'

Toby bristled. 'I'd fight him if necessary,' he declared.

'Fight him! What for?' Pinkie responded. 'The kittens?'

'Don't be foolish, Pinkie. You know very well what for.'

And Pinkie did know and she felt a twinge of excitement at this unlikely prospect. But she quickly said, 'I hope it never comes to a battle. It wouldn't be my wish. The kittens would never understand.'

'Oh, they'll soon be old enough to understand such

things,' Toby corrected her. 'Any you must realize that they'd most likely support me.'

Pinkie looked pained. It was all too true. 'I don't know why you're talking like this,' she said vexedly. 'You were always so sure Sammy had deserted me.'

Toby mumbled something to himself and jumped down from the wall. He was piqued by Pinkie's unreadiness to show her commitment to him. His attention was arrested by barking and yapping noises which became more agitated and angry as he listened. Pinkie leapt down and ran to the kittens.

'What's that?' she asked Toby.

'I don't know. I'll investigate. It's probably something happening in the meat yard.' He hurried away.

Pinkie instinctively shielded the kittens, although there was no indication that the trouble was likely to threaten them. Toby reappeared quite soon. 'Two of the dogs I told you about,' he summarised.

'What about them?'

'Fighting over scraps. Nothing to worry us. You should see the havoc they've caused. Bones and meat all over the yard. They must have ripped the containers to shreds.'

'Where did they come from?'

'They're household dogs that sometimes run on their own. They get underneath a gate into the yard from the street side. They're small animals but they look savage enough. They loathe each other.'

'The big black dog isn't around, is he?' Pinkie whispered.

'No. Haven't seen him since the time you came with me. I told you – he's a rare visitor.'

'All these dogs,' Pinkie commented anxiously. 'It frightens me at times.'

'Why should it? You don't need to encounter them. They're not going to come in here.'

'It was more peaceful in the park.'

'Was it?' Toby snapped. He was aggravated. 'What made you leave then?'

'Because of the kittens. They were uncomfortable. You know already.'

The barking and snarling reached a peak, then there was a piercing yelp of pain and finally the noise subsided.

'One of them's come out on top,' Toby explained wryly. 'I'll go back shortly and collect some of what they've left.'

When the butchers found their rubbish strewn all over the yard by the brawling dogs, they decided to replace the plastic sacks with metal bins – huge, heavy containers which were utterly beyond the scope or ingenuity of hungry cats to breach. Late one evening Toby recounted what he'd found. 'We'll have to move,' he said.

'Where to?'

'There's another place I know. It's in the open, but don't fret. It's safe enough.'

'No shelter?'

'There may be; I can't say for sure. I haven't visited it for a long time.'

'How far is it?'

'Well, quite a trek from here but the kittens can walk now. We'll need to go in the dead of night.'

'Yes, but the kittens have never strayed further than the boundaries of this yard,' Pinkie protested. 'They know nothing else.'

'High time they did, then,' was Toby's opinion.

Pinkie wailed. 'I don't like the prospect of this at all. Why don't we go to the park instead of this place you know? It's much closer and the ground's dried out a good deal. We could make ourselves –'

'No!' Toby interruped sharply. 'That wouldn't suit me

at all. I prefer my own haunts and so you must come where *I* say.'

'Oh. Must I? I don't quite see it that way,' Pinkie replied with quiet determination.

'You agreed to stick by me if I helped provide for you and your young ones.'

'And I have. But I'm not sure I can keep to that promise – if there's to be no shelter . . .'

'Well?'

'I must find my own. In the park.'

'I don't think you'll find that your best plan,' Toby said. There was a chill in his voice.

Pinkie looked at him steadily. Was there a threat implied by his words? She couldn't be sure.

'And how will you find enough food?' he asked in his more usual tone.

'I'll manage. I did before.'

'You won't do as well as you could with me.'

'Maybe.'

'Oh, you're not being sensible at all,' he said angrily. 'And don't be surprised if I find ways of compelling you to come with me.' He stalked away, leaving Pinkie to interpret his remark as best she might.

Pinkie quaked. She looked at the kittens who were tumbling around her legs unaware of the tension between the two adult cats. She realized she had probably made a mistake in forming a bond with Toby whose friendliness only seemed to operate on his terms. What would he do now? She couldn't imagine what his talk of compulsion meant. She knew only that she had to think first and foremost of her kittens and their safety, and if that also involved making them safe from *him*, there was no time to lose.

She looked around. Toby had left the yard. She had no way of knowing how far he had gone but this could be her only chance to get away. She ran to the end of the yard. The kittens followed her. The wall was a great difficulty because she would have to carry Moss, Fern and Little Sammy over it, one by one. She turned to the youngsters.

'Listen to me,' she said. 'I'm going to carry each of you over this wall. I'll take Fern first. Moss and Little Sammy – you must wait here and not make a sound until I come back for you. I shan't be long. And stay right here by the wall. Don't go wandering off.'

The little creatures gazed at their mother with big round eyes, impressed by the urgency in her voice.

'Right, come on, Fern,' Pinkie said and grasped her firmly by her neck fur. She leapt up the wall and over to the park side. It was quite a way to the shrubbery where the kittens had been born, but Pinkie knew it would be faster if she carried the kitten. She ran, feeling the weight of Fern pulling at her jaw, neck and shoulder muscles. The kittens had all grown considerably since she had last had to move them. All the time as she ran she wondered if Toby was lying in wait for her somewhere. But Pinkie made the first trip without mishap, leaving Fern hidden away once more amongst the thick stands of bamboo.

Moss and Little Sammy had been as good as gold. They had pressed themselves to the park wall and Pinkie found them together, silently shivering. Moss was next to go and Pinkie was greatly relieved that Toby so far showed no signs of interfering. She cautioned Little Sammy once more and set off.

She dropped Moss next to Fern. The two sister kittens mewed comfortably to each other as they snuggled down in the dry leaf litter. Pinkie turned again. One more trip and the kittens would be safe. She was half-way across the open space of the park when she heard sounds that made her blood run cold. Two deep echoing barks boomed in the far distance behind her. Her immediate thought was of the great black dog. She crouched, her heart thudding, and listened. There was another bark, closer this time. Pinkie was torn between returning to her daughters and racing on to rescue Little Sammy who was all on his own by the yard wall. She actually cried aloud in her anguish. It was almost impossible to think clearly. She was very exposed herself but she tried to reason that if the dog was indeed approaching, it was probably in search of food and would have no interest in her. Then she remembered the butcher's yard and Toby's description of how it had changed. What would the dog do if it found no food there? She shuddered and began to run. It was imperative that she fetch Little Sammy.

She reached the park wall again and, as she prepared to jump, she saw the huge black dog. It bounded across the open spaces with the most impressive speed and agility. Nothing, no animal that she had ever seen could have outrun it – not even a rabbit. Its stride was tremendous and, as she watched, the dog reached the wall behind the butcher's yard. Its mouth was agape and a long tongue dangled from its jaws. With one graceful movement the dog vaulted over the wall and, just for a second, Pinkie saw its glittering eye, caught by the starlight. She waited a moment longer. The dog's inevitable disappointment would make the animal even more dangerous.

She stole back for her remaining kitten. But Little Sammy was gone! Pinkie sprinted to the kittens' sleeping-box, calling him desperately. He was not there either. She began a frantic search of the yard, all the time terrified that the massive black hound would suddenly loom up behind her. The dog's furious howls of frustration pierced the silence as it discovered there was no meat. Pinkie was beside herself with anguish. Little Sammy had vanished and suddenly she guessed the reason. In her absence Toby must have returned and, either as punishment or as a means of persuading her to come back, had carried him off. There was no hope of finding him. Toby's new base was unknown to her. She had left her other kittens defenceless. How could she hope to save them if that hungry great beast should by chance head in their direction? Once again Pinkie was friendless and unsure about what to do for the best.

She couldn't stay where she was. The black dog's furious howls had ceased. It was turning its attention elsewhere. Despite her fears, the little white cat had to know its intentions. She sprang to the top of the wall and squatted there, panting. Almost at once the great dog emerged. It hurled itself over the wall, then braked to a halt. From the corner of its eye it had noticed Pinkie cringing against the coping. It stared at her and, amazingly, gave a feeble wag of its tail. With the utmost misery it boomed, 'No food! No food!' Then it turned and galloped away without a backward glance, as if by sheer pace and energy it could obliterate its exasperation. Here was no monster but only a fellow creature suffering familiar distress. Pinkie felt a degree of sympathy for the animal. Now she had no option but to return to her remaining kittens. She knew it could not be long before Toby would seek her out.

Go north!

Sammy, in the Embankment Gardens, had tried talking to the pigeons. The birds, of course, kept their distance. They were not going to be tricked into any trap by a cat. They were flustered by his presence in their feeding grounds and the last thing any one of them wanted to do was to allow the animal close enough to hold a conversation. Sammy was getting nowhere. There was only one way to get information out of them. He must catch one and make it talk. For a long time he circled the area, trying to spot a pigeon that was a little slower or a little older than its fellows. The human figures, wrapped cosily in their overcoats enjoying the winter sunshine, continued to supply the pigeons with crusts. From time to time they cast a wary eye on Sammy whom they hadn't seen before. They were distrustful of the cat, concerned as they apparently were for the birds' welfare. Sammy kept well away from the lunchers. He distrusted them as fervently as they did him.

Eventually, as lunch hours drew to a close, groups of people began to disperse. The gardens were soon empty, save for the cat and the birds. The pigeons and a few sparrows competed for the last few crumbs scattered around the seats. Sammy crawled underneath one of the wooden benches and watched the birds' squabbles. The pigeons forgot about him. He wriggled closer. Inevitably one of the birds strayed too close and Sammy was on to it before it knew what was happening. He was careful not to crush it or injure it too severely because he wanted this pigeon to live. His grip was just tight enough to prevent its escape.

'I'm not going to kill you,' he said coolly, 'and in fact you've nothing to fear from me as long as you do what I want.'

The pigeon had received such a shock it was unable to utter a sound.

'What I want from you is some assistance,' Sammy went on. 'You simply have to tell me how to get to the canal.'

The pigeon was silent.

'Do you know where it is?'

The pigeon blinked.

'Look, you're not helping yourself much,' Sammy rasped, irritated by the bird. 'I shan't release you if you won't co-operate. Now. Let's try again. Do you perhaps know where the park is?'

The captive pigeon stirred slightly but was unable to recover its composure sufficiently to talk. However, Sammy was encouraged. He relaxed his grip just a fraction. 'You *are* a Trafalgar Square pigeon, I suppose?' he muttered, half to himself.

'N-no,' the pigeon suddenly gasped. 'I'm – not. You've got the – wrong bird.'

Sammy seethed. It was too late to start all over again. The other birds had, of course, scattered immediately he had pounced on this one. His anger almost persuaded him to kill after all, but that would have gained him nothing except a meal. He restrained himself with difficulty. 'Very well,' said Sammy. 'Show me the way to Trafalgar Square. I have to consult with your friends there. If I let you go, will you fly off in the direction I must take?'

'Yes, yes, anything,' the pigeon gabbled. 'W-watch me. I'll indicate the way. You must find the island surrounded by roads.'

Sammy eased his claws back and the pigeon instantly flapped furiously, and soared upwards. Then it made a turn and, with Sammy following its flight intently, it winged its way towards the square. The tabby retired to the shrub border to wait until nightfall, satisfied that at last he had something to go on.

During the evening, overcome by hunger, Sammy raided the litter bins that were spaced at intervals around the gardens. He swallowed anything that was remotely edible and promised himself that the next day he would find some real food. As he did the rounds of human debris he had the distinct feeling he was being followed. When he looked behind he could see nothing, yet the feeling persisted. He paused to eat some stale bread and was astonished to hear a miaow of greeting. Sammy's head swivelled round and he saw Phoebe trotting across the dark grass towards him.

'You haven't got very far,' she commented.

Sammy explained he was about to move on. Then he asked, 'What are you doing here?'

Phoebe didn't reply at once. Then she said, 'I suppose I came to see if you'd caught anything.'

'But you didn't know I was here?'

'No.'

'Are you still hungry?'

'I'm always hungry.'

'So am I,' said Sammy. 'I'm afraid there's not much on offer here, but you're welcome to what you find. I'm going on now.'

'Oh. Are you?' She sounded just a mite disappointed.

'I have to, Phoebe. I'm sorry to leave you behind again.' Sammy was half hoping she would decide to accompany him but she said nothing. 'Well, goodbye again. And good luck,' said Sammy.

'Good luck to you.' Phoebe watched his departure and noted his route.

Sammy ambled up Northumberland Avenue towards Trafalgar Square. He kept in the shadows as much as he could. If he had been impressed before by the noise and bustle of London, he was stunned now by the cacophony and dazzled by the lights. How could he calmly walk into the midst of the tumult? He couldn't. He would have to exercise patience and trust that, later on, things would quieten down. Besides, no bird would be active in the middle of the night. He knew enough about birds' habits to be aware that they would all be roosting high up in trees or buildings beyond his reach. So he found a sheltered doorway and curled himself up. The air had turned very cold and Sammy wrapped his tail round his nose.

It wasn't until the early dark hours of the morning that the city seemed to sleep. Sammy stirred, stretched, and continued on his way at a brisk pace, trying to warm himself. The avenue ended and the tabby stood looking at the maze of roads that diverged from all sides and ran round the broad island in their midst. This island indeed appeared to be the only safe haven and Sammy crossed to it as soon as he was sure his way was clear. He had no doubt that he had arrived at the place called Trafalgar Square. He wandered about, looking for signs of life. It was still too dark for any bird to make an appearance.

He sat by the steps at the base of Nelson's Column and began to think just how ridiculous the whole notion was of a cat trying to talk to a bird. There could be a thousand birds in Trafalgar Square, but none of them would want to get within his reach. How on earth was he to proceed ? As he sat contemplating, flakes of snow began to fall softly, melting as they brushed his fur. Sammy looked up. The sky was lightening and, in the absence of the slightest breeze, the flakes drifted down vertically. He gazed up at the immensely tall column and on it he caught sight of a row of grey huddled bodies, pressed together on a ledge. These were the very pigeons he had come to consult.

Sammy acted promptly. He called up to them, 'Who can tell me how to find the canal?'

Some of the birds shifted on their perch and peered down at him, ruffling their feathers. None of them could imagine it was they who were being addressed by a cat, and therefore none of them answered.

'You pigeons!' Sammy cried. 'Tell me which way to go and I'll leave you in peace.'

The birds cooed questioningly to each other. Most of them hadn't an inkling of what Sammy was talking about and they naturally had no desire to get into conversation with a cat. But one wise pigeon could see it would be advisable to play the animal's game and get him away from the area as quickly as possible.

'Canal, did you say?' it trilled at Sammy. 'You must go north, go north.' It did have some notion of the direction.

'North? Which way is that?'

'Turn about and face the other way. Yes – that's right. Now, *that's* north. Hold that direction throughout and you will reach your goal.'

Sammy was inclined to be suspicious. It sounded a little too simple. But he was in no position to argue and he accepted the advice for what it was worth. He began to walk away from the column, towards the side of the square where the National Gallery stands. And the minute he did so he had a strange feeling. It felt *right* to him that he should be taking this direction, as if in a way Pinkie and his destination had suddenly come closer.

And the fact was, he *was* going the right way. Quite by chance the pigeon had set him on the correct route.

Of course Sammy believed that, some time later that day, he would find the park and the canal before him, and thus his travels would be over. But it wasn't as easy as that. He had a long way to go through an entirely built-up area; roads to negotiate, people to beware of, traffic to avoid and huge blocks of buildings to skirt.

He ran along a path by the National Gallery but his way was barred almost at once by a row of high buildings. He turned to see how he might pass them. He ran to the corner of the lane where it joined St Martin's Street, made a right turn at the edge of the block and was once more heading north. Moments later he was in Leicester Square.

The city still slumbered. Snow sifted down, forming a thin glistening carpet over the pavements and roads. The air was icy but crisp and Sammy felt invigorated. He thought constantly of Pinkie and how she must have given him up long ago. He pictured her wonder and excitement when he suddenly appeared, like a returning hero, full of tales of his adventures. He had been through so many changes he had scarcely had time to consider whether he had missed her. But now, when he felt he must be so close to rejoining her, he realized he had missed her a great deal.

Sammy progressed through Leicester Square. The square, usually so throbbing with life, was now all but deserted. He was becoming accustomed to the fact that a solitary cat, ranging through the streets, was of little interest to the handful of the city's human population who were out and about at that hour. Starlings who had roosted in the tree-tops and buildings of the square were waking and calling to each other. The sky lightened bit by bit but the snow clouds blanketed the sky, veiling the rising sun. The city was astonishingly quiet under the gathering carpet of snow. Sammy progressed north of the square. Diverted by another row of buildings, he reached Wardour Street. An old drunk, sitting against the wall of a narrow passage, called to him, but Sammy slipped past, nimble and silent.

Shaftesbury Avenue was the next obstacle. A taxi passed and then the tabby pattered across and, continuing straight ahead, resumed his path along Wardour Street. It was now light enough for Sammy to consider finding shelter. Odours of food from the litter around the deserted Berwick Street Market attracted him. He allowed his nose to guide him. The decaying vegetable matter from the greengrocery stalls was of no interest. However, he found a rich harvest of discarded takeaway kebab and hamburger cartons. Scraps of meat and ice-cold chips were all grist to the mill of his hunger. Raw meat and fat from a butcher's premises and a few prawn skins from a fishmonger's added to the variety. He ate everything that he could find and, for the first time in days, his hunger was satisfied. A puddle that hadn't completely frozen over quenched his thirst. Then he got under one of the market barrows, hiding behind the covering tarpaulin, with the intention of sleeping through the daylight hours. As London started another day Sammy nodded and slept, dreaming fitfully of Pinkie and their old life in Quartermile Field.

—14—

Mother love

While Sammy dreamed of her, Pinkie, curled up with Moss and Fern in the bamboo stand, was watching the snowflakes falling through her screen of leaves. She longed to know where her other kitten was and to have him restored to her protection.

As she had expected, Toby came looking for her early that morning. She heard his calls rasping persistently in the clear air. Reluctantly she answered him. Toby came running eagerly, his paws leaving a trail of prints in the fresh snow.

'I bring news for you,' he said with satisfaction, butting his way through the shrub stems. 'Your kitten is safe.'

Pinkie looked at him coldly, pressing herself closer against Moss and Fern. 'Where is he?' she demanded. 'Where is Little Sammy?'

'Don't alarm yourself, Pinkie. I'm looking after him.'

'*You*? How can you be looking after him when you're here talking to me?'

'Because I've made sure he's in a safe place.'

'How dare you carry off one of my little ones? You waited until I was out of the way and then –'

'Hush, hush, calm down,' Toby interrupted her. 'It wasn't like that at all. I found the little fellow cowering against the wall, completely unprotected. The black dog was loose – you must have heard it – so I didn't wait to see if you were coming back. I picked the kitten up and got him out of the way before any harm could be done. You should be grateful to me.'

'I'm grateful he came to no harm,' Pinkie replied, 'but that great dog is nothing but a half-starved brute after all. Now, where have you taken Little Sammy?'

Toby looked cunning. 'Come and see for yourself.'

'No. I can't move my other kittens again. The weather's worsening. We need to stay put. You must bring Little Sammy to me.'

'I can't do that,' said Toby craftily.

'You can and you must. You've no right to keep him from me.'

'Maybe not, Pinkie, but it's you who are choosing not to re-unite your little family. I told you before, I wouldn't live in this park. I prefer my own territory. If I bring Little Sammy here, you and I would be separated for good. I don't want that. I don't want that at all.'

'So you want to use my kitten to keep a hold over me?'

'That's not how I see it. If you'd only be sensible, we could all be comfortable together again. What is there here for you? The park is open and exposed, not like the place Little Sammy and I are using. Think about it. What will your precious park be like laden with snow?'

Pinkie didn't answer this. Instead she asked a question. 'Are you feeding him? He's barely weaned.'

'He eats anything he's given. He won't starve. But he wants you to come back.'

'Does he say so?'

'The odd word. Mother, Moss, Fern – it's all he knows, isn't it?'

'Oh, you are a tormentor!' Pinkie cried. 'How can you torture me like this?'

'I don't wish to. Will you come then?'

'Not while the snow's falling. It's not a time to ferry kittens about.'

Toby seized on this. He said slyly, 'Then how can you expect me to bring Little Sammy through the snow?'

'Oh, you think you're very smart don't you? Why do you stay here bantering like this? I'd rather you got back to your own favourite lair or whatever you have and watch over my stolen kitten. How do you know he hasn't wandered off while you've been wasting time with me?'

'He won't have. He listens to me. I told him not to stray.'

'*Did* you?' Pinkie hissed jealously. 'You'd like to usurp me, wouldn't you? *I'm* his parent, not you!'

'Of course you are,' Toby said sweetly, 'and that's why I'm surprised you want to stay here without him.'

'I don't want to!' Pinkie screeched. 'Oh, get away from me, you hateful cat. To think I ever put my faith in you!'

Toby retreated. He had made his point and reckoned it was enough for Pinkie to brood upon. He was certain she'd soon feel so uneasy about Little Sammy that she would be powerless to resist his suggestion. He planned to stay away for a day or two to allow her mother's conscience to get to work.

However, for the present, Pinkie had other things to think about, the most vital of which was food. Moss and Fern were hungry and she had nothing to give them. She quickly recalled the gifts of food so regularly brought to the park by the young woman, Lizzie Reed. Pinkie had relied on them before, now she would have to do so again. How could she know that these supplies had ceased since her earlier disappearance from the park?

The little white mother cat stirred and stood up. Moss and Fern instantly felt the cruel change in temperature as Pinkie's warmth was removed from them. They began to protest.

'Don't fret, kittens,' their mother told them. 'I have to fetch food. We all need to eat.' She scraped a pile of dry dead leaves around them. It was the best she could do. 'Burrow into these,' she said. 'They'll help to keep the chill out.' She left them and trotted into the open. The snow continued to fall. Pinkie enjoyed the soft feel of it underfoot and she tripped along briskly. It was very early and, except for the waterfowl on the partly frozen lake, she felt as if she was the only creature about. She looked in the usual places for the scraps. Of course there weren't any. Pinkie sat under the shelter of an evergreen shrub and waited. She knew that humans roused themselves later and she watched eagerly for their arrival.

There were few visitors to the park that morning, and those who did brave the weather failed to notice Pinkie whose coat was almost indistinguishable from the white mass that surrounded her. The familiar figure of Lizzie Reed, the food-bringer, didn't appear.

'I can't return without *something*,' Pinkie said to herself. She looked around. Ducks, geese and swans paddled in the patches of unfrozen water. Some stood awkwardly on the slippery ice, looking puzzled and uncomfortable. They were too big and strong for her to catch. And with snow covering the ground, food-gathering for the smaller birds was all but impossible. They stayed in the bushes or tree-tops, out of Pinkie's reach.

'There's nothing to hunt,' she muttered. 'It looks as if the litter-bins are my only hope.'

She soon discovered that these were empty. Yesterday's rubbish had been collected. The park seemed devoid of sustenance. Pinkie thought of Toby. *He* was finding food. Her pride wavered. She had to be practical. She hurried back to Moss and Fern.

The kittens jumped up to greet her. They nuzzled her and uttered little squeaky miaows, begging for food.

'There's no food yet,' Pinkie told them regretfully. 'But there will be soon. I'm going to look for Toby. He can help.'

'Toby, Toby,' chanted the kittens. His name was one of the first things they had learnt.

'Yes, you'd both be full of praise for him, I suppose, if you could say more,' their mother remarked. 'But you don't really know him. He isn't quite the friend you think he is.'

To the kittens' dismay, Pinkie disappeared again. Moss ran after her a little way but she was soon left behind. Fern called her sister plaintively and Moss turned back, skipping through the powdery snow and trying to pounce on the snowflakes as they landed. She wanted to play and she frisked about, chasing her tail and tumbling over herself. Fern watched avidly and was soon persuaded to join in. So, while their mother was absent, believing them to be securely hidden, the kittens played out in the open, oblivious of any danger.

Pinkie sought Toby beyond the park. She walked precariously along the slippery coping of the wall, calling him and looking into each yard. Her search was hopeless. Toby had returned to his other hideaway where he had taken Little Sammy. But she did have one piece of luck. Under the snow-covered climbing stems of the ivy, where Toby had once hidden some sausages, she found some pieces of meat, neglected or forgotten by the grey tom who had now moved his quarters. Because of the cold the meat hadn't rotted. In any case Pinkie was quite used to high-tasting carrion from her earliest days, so she looked upon this little store as providential. There was enough for her and her kittens for a day or two. Toby hadn't beaten her yet.

She took up the largest chunk she could carry and

hastened away. She approached her bamboo den from the rear. It was now mid-morning. Moss and Fern were nowhere to be seen. Their leaf-litter nest was deserted. Pinkie dropped the meat and rushed into the open. And there were the kittens, still enjoying their games and now surrounded by a group of humans with rapt expressions on their shining faces. Pinkie hesitated. She had never put any trust in humans. They were there to make use of when necessary, that's all. She couldn't tell if her kittens were at risk or not. The kittens themselves had no experience of people and, being so caught up in their games, were simply unaware of their interest.

Pinkie called nervously. The kittens didn't hear, they were far too busy. Their fur was daubed with semi-melted snow and they continued to chase each other around, squealing in delight. Pinkie called again, more urgently. Moss and Fern paused and looked about them. They saw their mother and ran to her excitedly. But Pinkie was in a hurry to get to safety. Scolding her youngsters, she nipped each of them in the rear and shepherded them directly to the den. The onlookers understood now where the fluffy little kittens had come from. They were the offspring of strays they told each other, commenting on the sad plight of such animals exposed to all conditions of weather. As the little crowd broke up and dispersed, two or three of its members made a mental note of where the animals had hidden themselves. It was their express intention to come back with some treat or other to help them through the winter.

Meanwhile mother and daughters were devouring the half-frozen meat from Toby's abandoned store. Pinkie softened and fragmented the chunks first with her own teeth before passing morsels to the kittens. There was enough for all of them. Pinkie waited for Moss and Fern to be satisfied before she ate her own share. Then she said,

'Don't ever move from here again when I'm not with you. You could have been stolen from me. I've already lost one kitten and I don't want to lose any more.'

She made sure the youngsters understood and then she began to think again about Little Sammy. She was determined to get him back, but in her own way. She guessed Toby would be back to try his persuasion all over again. She would spurn him, but then follow him secretly when he left her. Let *him* lead her to his new hideout.

Pinkie was right. The next day, at dusk, Toby came looking for her. She had just returned with some more of the meat from the forgotten store, and the grey tom arrived to see Pinkie and the kittens enjoying what looked to him like a substantial meal. He was a little put out by the sight.

'That looks like butcher's meat,' he commented. 'But how can you still be getting that?'

Pinkie took time to answer, chewing elaborately on a large mouthful. 'I can fend for myself,' she declared. 'I can see you're surprised by it. But I must look after my kittens.'

'That's what I've come about,' Toby growled.

'I thought as much.'

'Well, have you changed your mind?'

'No! As you can see, the park has all I need. You won't entice me away, so you may as well accept it and bring Little Sammy back.'

Toby was baffled by her obstinacy. He lost his temper. 'You'll never see him again,' he threatened her. 'Not unless you accompany me.'

'You've had your answer to that,' she reminded him acidly, angry in her turn.

'Is this your last word?'

'You can count on it.'

'A fine mother you are to your kittens,' Toby snarled.

Pinkie could see it would be in her interest to pretend not to care about Little Sammy. Then Toby would have little cause to suspect she'd follow him. 'I'm fully occupied with these two without having to worry about their brother all the time,' she told him airily. 'Especially when you assure me,' she added mischievously, 'you're taking such good care of him.'

Toby blinked at her. He couldn't believe his ploy had failed. 'You've changed your attitude a good deal,' he muttered. He sounded defeated.

'I've had to,' Pinkie answered. 'You've seen to that.'

Toby turned away, brushing snow from the leaves as he passed and showering himself generously. But he was oblivious of such discomfort. He reckoned that he had lost Pinkie for good and, morose, and angry with himself more than with her, he left without another word.

Pinkie settled her kittens. Moss and Fern listened to her instructions. 'I'm going in search of your brother,' their mother told them. 'You're not to move from here, do you understand? Remember what I said before; it's dangerous. You're to wait here until I come back. I may be quite some time but, as long as you stay put, you'll be entirely safe.' She pulled some sprigs of fir around them which she had scraped together from the shrubbery bottom. The kittens were well concealed, dry, and sheltered from the cold. Pinkie skipped away with one last look back.

Ahead of her, Toby approached the park entrance, the very place where Pinkie and Sammy had entered so many weeks before. Pinkie stole along in his wake, a white blur against the snow. She stayed just far enough behind the grey tom to keep him in view, but to avoid attracting his attention. When he paused, she paused; when he moved on, she moved on. Toby stopped at the wide street Pinkie and Sammy had crossed to reach the park. Pinkie hung back, wondering where he would go next. To her astonishment, Toby sat patiently by the kerb, glancing left and right at the noisy traffic.

'He's going to cross that road, I know it,' Pinkie whispered to herself. 'Oh dear, I don't think I can go after him.' Then she gave herself a shake. 'Of course I can. I've got to, for Little Sammy's sake. I did it before, I'll do it again.'

Pinkie's fears were realized. Toby saw a gap and sprinted across. Pinkie trotted to the pavement. She saw Toby running ahead, up the other side of the road to a side turning. Something about that particular turning was familiar. She was sure she and Sammy had come from that side road after they had escaped from the removal van. She stood at the edge of the kerb, her heart beating painfully. She remembered how she and Sammy had taken refuge under a vehicle. She did the same now. From under a parked lorry's protective hulk she watched for her opportunity. Traffic streamed past. It seemed to her as though there would never be an end to it. Then, at long last, she saw her chance and raced over, gaining the opposite pavement just before a taxi sped by. She actually felt the vehicle brush her tail, so narrow was her escape. But, frightened as she was, she couldn't stop to think about that. She had to stay on Toby's trail.

She turned the corner. Yes, this was where she and Sammy had taken their first few steps into the heart of this new environment. She saw Toby clearly in the snow-covered lane just before he disappeared through an opening in a wall. Pinkie had a shrewd idea what that opening would lead to. She slunk cautiously along the wall and, as she reached the opening, she stopped and poked just her head round. The yard gates of the removal firm's premises were ahead of her, flung wide to admit their returning lorries and . . . Toby! Pinkie saw him creep underneath one of the huge vehicles. There were no men about in the yard. There was a small office building which was lit up and she saw a man on his own moving round inside. Pinkie crept into the yard and hid behind one of the lorry's wheels. She was back where she had started. She heard some miaowing coming from the front end of the vehicle. She knew at once it was Toby talking to Little Sammy. Keeping herself hidden, Pinkie moved closer.

'Your mother positively refuses to come,' Toby was saying. 'She's given you up. She doesn't seem to want you any more. Don't ask me why. My plan's backfired on me.' There was silence for a moment. Pinkie's heart ached. Then Toby resumed, 'I don't expect you understand a word I'm saying to you?'

Pinkie next heard Little Sammy's squeaky voice. 'Mother – not – coming,' he repeated with difficulty.

'Oh, I'm coming, I'm coming, you'll see,' she whispered inaudibly. Her heart was overflowing.

'Did the men give you your food?' Toby asked next.

'Yes.'

'Is there any left?'

'Yes, there's – there's – p-lenty.'

'Good boy. You're learning fast. We get along all right, don't we? Never mind your mother.'

Pinkie saw Toby move away and then she noticed that, against the wall of the little office, there was a food-bowl which the grey tom was investigating. She ran to the front of the lorry. Little Sammy was curled up underneath. The ground was quite dry where the lorry had prevented the snow from settling.

'Quick! Up!' Pinkie hissed in a tone of command. 'While his back's turned.'

Little Sammy, overjoyed at seeing his mother who belied the unwelcome news he had just heard, hastened to her side. He wasn't equipped to deal with contradictions.

He only knew Pinkie was there and that her tongue was licking his face fur in that wonderful motherly way he remembered from his earliest hours. Then she seized him by his neck fur and, minutes later, they were out of the yard and away along the lane, mother carrying son and moving as fast as she could go, back in the direction of the park.

But Pinkie wasn't thinking just about her refuge in the park. She was a step ahead of that and in her mind she pictured herself and her kittens not in the park, but in Quartermile Field. She really thought she had found the clue to her return there. The sight of the removal van, parked in the yard where she and Sammy had come to rest after their long journey, had stimulated her memory. If the van had brought them here from the neighbourhood of their old home, why couldn't it take her back again? And with her kittens? To Pinkie the logic of this idea was faultless. In a few more weeks the kittens would be ready to walk greater distances. There would be no more carrying to be done. Then they could follow their mother wherever she led them. And Pinkie meant to lead them to their real home.

15

You're going to
see your father

Pinkie and Little Sammy reached the end of the lane
without any trouble. Pinkie set the kitten down against the
wall. Little Sammy rubbed himself against his mother
affectionately and began asking about Moss and Fern.

'You'll soon see them,' his mother assured him. She cast
a glance behind to see if Toby was coming. No, the lane
was clear. Now she thought about the busy street. 'Before
we get home we have to put ourselves in some danger,' she
said, recalling her narrow escape from the taxi. 'Whatever
you do – however scared you are – *don't move*. I'm going to
carry you across a wide frightening road. You've been
across it with Toby but you may not remember, as it
wouldn't have been so full of frightening things then.'

Little Sammy's eyes were popping. Pinkie grabbed him
and moved out into the main street. The sight that greeted
her was of a road chock-a-block with rush-hour traffic.
However, there was one consolation for Pinkie. The
congestion in the road was such that, at the moment they
reached the pavement edge, there was a temporary
standstill. Pinkie was quick to notice. She didn't linger
but, weaving her way boldly between and around the
vehicles, she managed to get three quarters of the way

across before it began to edge forward again. She couldn't turn back. Terrified that at any moment she would be knocked flat, she had to keep on going. There was a squeal of brakes as she scampered in front of a car, but the driver was able to avoid the cat and her kitten and, before he had thoroughly recovered his wits, the animals were safe on the pavement and Pinkie was running lickety-split for the park entrance with her live bundle bumping against her chest.

Inside the peace and quiet of the park she set Little Sammy down. 'We've survived,' she gasped. 'It's a miracle.'

She allowed Little Sammy to walk the rest of the way himself. He trotted after Pinkie gamely. He hardly knew what danger he had been in and he was far more interested in the way his little feet sank into the soft powdery snow at each step.

As they approached their den, Pinkie experienced a strange sensation which made her stop dead in her tracks. She could feel as plainly as though she could see him, that Sammy, her long-lost mate, was coming back. She sensed that he was closer to her than he had been for a long time. 'Your father,' she whispered wonderingly to Little Sammy, 'you're going to see your father.'

And Sammy *was* on the move again. He had been rudely awakened by the noise and bustle of the market. The barrow he had chosen as a shelter was reclaimed and the stall-owner began to dress it with produce to sell. Sammy felt vulnerable amid the stamping feet and the blows and buffets of the cart. He slipped away in the morning rush and was hastened on his way by the market fishmonger who didn't want a grubby tabby sniffing after his wares.

Sammy ran and hid in a doorway. Then he recovered himself, remembered to set his face north, and ambled along Wardour Street looking for an alternative shelter to use until nightfall. He could find nothing permanent and he spent the rest of the day under parked cars or in doorways, moving from one spot to another as necessary.

When it grew dark Sammy continued north. A solitary cat such as he went unremarked amongst the throngs of people hurrying home. He slunk along, avoiding the rush, and made good progress until he reached the nightmare of Oxford Street. This was no place for a cat. Sammy turned tail and fled. But he brought himself to a sudden halt. This wouldn't do. He was going back on himself. He remembered the pandemonium in Trafalgar Square and how, when he had been patient, this had eventually died down. He must do the same this time. He sat against a shopfront, closed his eyes and dozed; but not for long. The cold, the tramp of feet and his own eagerness to be reunited with Pinkie wouldn't allow him to sleep.

In the early hours he crossed Oxford Street, continued along Berners Street and then into Cleveland Street. Now there was another wide road to negotiate, but Sammy was becoming an old hand now. He sprinted across Euston Road, made some turns and was in Albany Street by daylight. He was very tired. Across to his left he saw trees. This seemed to him a good sign. He headed for them and scrambled under a hedge, utterly exhausted. He was on the borders of Regent's Park.

This time Sammy did sleep, and he slept for a long time. The day was well on when he awoke. He was stiff and thoroughly chilled but when he looked up, these feelings were quickly forgotten. Sitting about a metre away, regarding him steadily, was Phoebe.

Sammy jumped up. 'How did you –? What on earth have you –?' he spluttered.

'I shadowed you,' she answered simply.

'When? How? It seems I've been travelling for ages.'

'I was never far behind you,' said Phoebe. 'You never suspected then?'

'Of course not. How could I have? All this way!'

'Yes, all this way, Sammy.'

He looked long and hard at her. 'But why? I don't understand.'

'I thought you needed a companion but . . . well, I was never quite sure. I kept my distance. Then, when you looked as if you'd reached your journey's end, I had to come into the open.'

Sammy was perplexed. He didn't know what Phoebe expected of him and he didn't know how to react. 'I – I haven't reached the end of my journey,' he said uncertainly. 'Not yet. I have to find the canal, you see, in order to get my bearings. I have to go north.'

'Shall we go then? Are you fully rested? I'm quite fresh. But you must need to eat.'

'You're so right,' Sammy agreed. 'We've travelled quite a distance, haven't we? And, you know, I'm beginning to feel I understand this place.'

'What place?'

'Well, this . . . I mean, all around here . . . the whole thing . . .' Sammy struggled to explain as they walked on.

'You mean the city?' Phoebe prompted.

'That's it – the city!' Sammy cried. 'I think I'm getting used to it. It was daunting at first but, after a while, I wasn't so scared. I think I've worked out how to deal with the roads, the noise, the people, the – the whole *hugeness* of it. You have to make yourself part of it, to – to – slip into its ways and then it's not so frightening in the end. Do you understand me?'

'Of course I do. I've lived in it all my life,' Phoebe replied. 'Now what about the food?'

The cats moved stealthily along the hedge-side. Their

footfalls were totally silent in the snow. But no further snow fell and the sun began to shine with real strength. Sammy and Phoebe were grateful for that little bit of extra warmth.

'I don't think we'll catch anything on this side of the park,' Phoebe commented as they crossed Chester Road.

Safely on the other side Sammy turned to her. 'Park?' he echoed, peering through the hedge border. 'Yes, of course! It *is* a park. But the snow has changed it and I can't be sure. This may be what I've been searching for,' he added excitedly. 'If there's a canal nearby, then I'm home.'

Phoebe began to think they never would get anything to eat. 'Look, why don't we go in?' she suggested. 'You can have a scout around and see if you recognize anything. And we should be able to find something to eat.'

They found their way into the park. Sammy was actually on the opposite side to where he and Pinkie had set up home near the lake. Under the hedge the tabby sniffed out some carrion. Two small birds had succumbed to the extreme cold overnight and now made the cats a frugal repast. The animals moved on.

'What will you do if you find your canal?' Phoebe asked suddenly. She'd been wondering where she might fit in with Sammy's future plans.

And Sammy hadn't given this a thought. Her question brought a problem into his mind. Supposing he *were* to find Pinkie soon? He had longed for that moment. But now there was Phoebe too. He could foresee difficulties. What *did* his present companion expect of him? She'd referred to his hunting prowess but, surely, finding food was only part of it? Was she really hoping for his company in the long term? He had to give her an answer.

'If I find the canal,' Sammy said slowly, 'I'll be able to return to my den.'

'Will it still be the same?'

'I don't know.' He looked at Phoebe. Their eyes met. 'You see, I had a mate,' he explained.

'Oh. You didn't mention that before?'

'No, I didn't see the need to, Phoebe. I didn't expect you to follow me.'

'No. I'm not quite sure myself why I've done it. Will your mate be around – I mean, there may be other cats?'

'I can't tell, Phoebe. Not till I've been back.'

They found some more carrion. The late flurry of winter weather had taken its toll. As they ate silently, Phoebe found herself wishing there would be no canal. When they had finished, Sammy, without a word, continued forward. His eagerness to be moving on was a disappointment to the black and white cat. She imagined Sammy was eager to be rid of her.

In places the snow was beginning to thaw. The paths were clear and easier to walk on. Sammy hurried over the snow-covered grass to a broad walkway where he was able to put on a spurt. Phoebe, dismayed, fell back a little, but kept him in view. Both cats kept well away from the few people walking through the park. Sammy in particular wanted nothing and no one to delay him now. But his sudden rush was unexpectedly halted.

Over on his left side he caught sight of an enclosure – a sort of pen with a high metal fence – which contained a large number of what he thought were dogs. He came to a stop, uncertain if they were securely caged. He didn't know he was looking at the enclosure of timber-wolves in London Zoo. The beasts trotted back and forth on springy legs. Some of them peered at Sammy with calculating looks in their eyes as if daring him to go on past. They were restless and looked very much in their element in the snow. One of them raised its head and howled. The sound was eerie but familiar. Sammy recognized it immediately. He had heard just such a howl that first night in the park with Pinkie. Was this then, the source of all those terrifying animal noises? He darted past the cage, sensing the wolves' green eyes boring into his back as he fled, certain that at any moment they would give chase. But, growing in Sammy's mind was the thought that he must have found his way back. The park, the animal cries. And then, suddenly, there it was – the gleam of water. Straight ahead of him lay the canal!

He turned to see if he was pursued. There were no wolves on his tail – only Phoebe, trotting along hesitantly, unsure whether or not to rejoin him. Sammy tarried. He had to show her the canal.

'I'm home, Phoebe,' he announced. 'I only have to follow the water till I get my bearings.'

'I wish you well,' the female cat whispered.

'If I find nothing,' Sammy said meaningfully, 'I'll come looking for you. Will you stay around?'

'Yes, I'll stay,' she answered. 'But come anyway, Sammy, whatever you find. I'd like to know about it.' She watched him depart for the canal bank and then, slowly but determinedly, she followed him, always keeping her distance but never losing sight of him, just as she had followed him across the breadth of London.

Pinkie nestled in the den with her three kittens. She had fetched food for them, collecting the generous offerings from those bystanders who had witnessed the female kittens playing. The cats had so much food that Pinkie had secreted some amongst the bushes in the shrubbery, conveniently close to the den. She recognized the rise in temperature and her hopes rose along with it of an end to the hard cold days.

Little Sammy, Moss and Fern, curled up comfortably around their mother, listened, enthralled, as she told them about their father. Pinkie was glad she had waited until they were all together to do this, and she knew that the kittens were old enough now to understand most of what she had to tell them. She told them about Quartermile Field and about Sammy's first appearance there. She told them how he had superseded his own father as leader of the vagabond cats and had become the King Cat. Then she explained how she and Sammy had paired off from the rest to make their own home; and how the other cats had left the area so that eventually she and Sammy had the whole of Quartermile Field to themselves. She told her family about Sammy's exploits and how the two of them had been carried away from their home by the strange machine, and then had escaped from it to make a new home in the park. In a softer voice she described how she thought she and Sammy had come to be separated. 'But he's coming back, he's coming back, I know it,' she finished in a whisper. 'And soon you're going to see him. What a surprise he will have, too, when he sees you!'

'Is he like Toby?' asked Little Sammy.

'No, he's nothing like him,' Pinkie said crossly. 'You must forget about Toby now. *He's* not part of our family at all.' She sighed and gazed out at the open park. 'In fact,' Pinkie added, 'I hope we never set eyes on him again.'

16

The fate of four cats

All morning Toby had been frantically searching around the removal yard. He thought Little Sammy had wandered off by himself and, as he had made himself responsible for the male kitten, he dreaded to think what Pinkie's reaction would be if she discovered that he hadn't taken proper care of him.

'I shan't tell her, I *can't* tell her,' Toby muttered to himself as he ran round, looking under lorries and into every corner of the yard. 'Oh, I blame myself! I shouldn't have left him alone. Kittens are very inquisitive; he was bound to go exploring some time . . . I didn't warn him sufficiently about the dangers. Poor Little Sammy!'

Of course the kitten was not found. Toby left the yard to continue his search outside in the lane. If he had gone along it straight away to the main street he might have been in time to see Pinkie carrying Little Sammy across. But he didn't – he went the other way, which he deemed was less threatening to a kitten. He went as far as he thought Little Sammy could have run on his own in the time since his disappearance. Then he turned back to look in the other direction.

'Surely he can't have wandered into the main street?' Toby murmured fearfully. 'The noise and din would be enough to drive him back. But, in that case, where is he?'

Toby spent a long time pacing up and down the street. All along, his mind had been occupied by the nightmare of finding the kitten's body in the gutter but, when he failed to see anything, he perked up a little. He managed to cross to the other side and renewed his search there.

'He must have survived,' he breathed thankfully, but his relief was tempered by the belief that, if Little Sammy wasn't killed, he was certainly lost.

'He couldn't have found his way back to his mother, could he?' Toby asked himself. 'If so I may be searching for nothing. Anyway I ought to investigate. But then . . . what if he isn't with Pinkie, whatever should I say to her? Oh, I don't know what to do!'

Toby bitterly regretted now that he had carried Little Sammy off in the first place. This ruse hadn't brought Pinkie back to him and, despite the fact that he was no relation to the kittens, Toby had become very fond of them. If any harm had come to Little Sammy because of his carelessness he would never forgive himself. He paced up and down indecisively. He dreaded confronting Pinkie but, at the same time, he had to put his mind at rest.

'Perhaps I'll see Little Sammy in the park,' he told himself, 'without being noticed myself.' He mused over this. 'Yes, it's worth a try,' he decided. 'I'll go cautiously, a bit at a time.'

He went a little way into the park and looked about. He saw no kitten, but instead an adult black and white cat walking towards the lake. Toby had never seen this animal before. He kept her in sight as he continued with his search. Phoebe observed the grey tom but otherwise ignored him. She had followed Sammy too far to be deterred now. As the tabby disappeared into the shrubbery, she sat down in the snow and waited.

In the midst of the stand of bamboo, Pinkie saw Sammy

approach. Despite her premonition she was overcome by
the sight of him after all these weeks. She purred deep in
her throat and the kittens, sensing her pleasure, began to
purr too.

'He's here, your father's here,' Pinkie whispered joyfully.

'Father's here, Father's here,' crowed the kittens.

Sammy burst into the den and stopped in amazement.
The tabby and white kittens came to greet him but
Sammy was so stunned he was unable to move or to offer
them a greeting.

'Pinkie!' he said hoarsely, believing the worst. 'Are
you . . . ?'

'They're yours; yours and mine,' she purred. 'Dear
Sammy, I all but gave you up.'

'I've so much to tell you,' he murmured, bending his
head to nuzzle his offspring. 'But this is the most
wonderful surprise. How old are they?'

Pinkie told him.

'Oh look,' said Sammy, 'they have both our colourings!
Oh, what I've been missing! But Pinkie, from the first day
I was taken, I have never stopped planning my return.
I've travelled as far as – as – well, let me just say, I've
traversed the city in search of you.'

Pinkie purred even louder and brushed against him,
butting him gently with her head and rubbing her muzzle
against his wet fur. 'You were taken?' she murmured.

'I was injured,' Sammy told her. 'A human rescued me.
She was kind and fed me and made me well but – I was
imprisoned. It was an age before I could escape.'

'You've grown thin,' Pinkie remarked.

'I was thinking the same about you,' Sammy told her.
'Have things been hard here?'

'Mostly. But we haven't been here all the time,' Pinkie
answered. 'I too have a story to tell. There was – um –
another cat.'

'Oh!' Sammy was reminded immediately of Phoebe. 'I met another one, too. But that's not important now.' Phoebe seemed very distant now that Sammy had his family all purring contentedly around him. 'What do you call them?' he murmured.

'Moss, Fern, and Little Sammy.'

'Oh-oh, I think I can guess which one's named after me,' Sammy joked, watching the stoutest of the kittens. 'And at least he hasn't got my ugly face.'

'Oh Sammy,' said Pinkie, 'what nonsense! You've always been a fine-looking cat. And I have missed you so.'

Sammy whispered, 'I dreamed of you.'

'Sammy, Sammy,' chanted the sisters. 'Tell us your adventures.'

'There's plenty of time for that,' said Pinkie. 'Let your father rest now. He's very tired and I must bring him some food from our store.'

Whilst Phoebe waited, Toby crept nearer to the shrubbery, a metre or two at a time. He was hoping to catch a glimpse of Little Sammy before Pinkie noticed him. But, Pinkie, her kittens, and now her mate, were all together in the den, more comfortable and content than they had been for a very long time. Toby slunk closer, straining his ears, his belly hugging the icy ground. He entered the shrubbery without a sound. The family of cats were so absorbed with each other they suspected nothing. Sammy ate with relish. And then, for the first time, Toby heard the tabby's voice.

'I can't rest just yet,' Sammy said, thinking of Phoebe. 'There's one more thing I have to do.'

Toby backed away clumsily, alarmed despite himself, and causing the evergreen shrub to rustle loudly.

'There's something out there,' Sammy said sharply and sallied forth from the den.

'I'm not losing sight of you again,' Pinkie said with resolve, and followed close behind him. In her wake, the kittens tumbled excitedly.

Toby saw everything – Little Sammy shepherding his smaller sisters, a determined Pinkie, and Sammy, the father of the family, with a challenge in his eyes. The grey tom fell back, aware he had invaded another's territory.

'Who are you?' demanded Sammy.

All previous thoughts of fighting for Pinkie's companionship vanished from Toby's head at the sight of this imperious male. He only acknowledged to himself that Little Sammy was where he should be and – to his deep personal regret – so was Pinkie.

'My name is Toby.'

'We were friends,' Pinkie explained with a triumphant gleam in her eyes as she noticed how Sammy had already cowed the grey tom.

Sammy turned to her. 'The other cat?' he enquired.

'Yes.' Pinkie tingled. Was there going to be a fight?

Sammy glared at Toby who had ceased to back away and was sitting on his haunches. The two males weighed each other up. Toby was ready to defend himself.

Suddenly, Moss and Fern began to chirp, 'Toby, Toby!' He was a more familiar figure to them than their father.

Pinkie was irritated and rounded on them. 'I thought I told you to forget Toby?' she hissed. The atmosphere was tense. Sammy and Toby stared at each other. The fur rose along their backs. Little Sammy, heeding his mother's words, sang out loyally, 'Sammy, Sammy!' Then, into this meeting of rivals, as if aware that the fate of four cats was to be decided, strolled Phoebe.

Toby barely gave her a glance but Sammy was taken aback by her sudden appearance and seemed to lose face. Now it was Pinkie's turn to bridle and her coat fluffed out. A growl began in her throat.

Sammy tried to collect herself. 'This is indeed a fateful day,' he muttered. He looked from Phoebe to Pinkie and back again, not quite sure how to master the situation. But Phoebe, like Toby, had seen all she had needed to see.

She said, 'So you found what you were looking for?'

Sammy replied quickly, 'Yes – and more. I've discovered I have extra responsibilities.'

Phoebe was content to withdraw. Sammy was in his rightful place and she accepted this. 'I'm glad for you,' she said simply. 'The kittens are lucky to have such a father.' She turned away. There was no more to be said. The tension eased.

Toby had no choice but to emulate Phoebe. His fate was mirrored in her departure. The bonds of family were stronger than ties of friendship. He walked away and, on an impulse, followed in Phoebe's tracks. Sammy and Pinkie exchanged fond looks. They caught Toby's first words to the black and white cat.

'I don't think I've seen you in this area before? Do you plan to stay?'

The reply was inaudible.

Sammy said, 'The snow's melting. Winter's almost over. In the spring we'll move to new quarters.'

Pinkie thought of the removal van, the great machine that had brought them to the city, and of how they could make use of it to take them back again. But she didn't need to think about that now.

'Whatever you say, Sammy,' she murmured. 'For I've learnt one thing – wherever we go it's you that will make it Home.'

Sammy gave her an affectionate glance. 'We'll decide it together,' he promised, 'for the good of our kittens.'

Other great reads *from* **Red Fox**

Discover the great animal stories of Colin Dann

JUST NUFFIN

The Summer holidays loomed ahead with nothing to look forward to except one dreary week in a caravan with only Mum and Dad for company. Roger was sure he'd be bored.

But then Dad finds Nuffin: an abandoned puppy who's more a bundle of skin and bones than a dog. Roger's holiday is transformed and he and Nuffin are inseparable. But Dad is adamant that Nuffin must find a new home. Is there *any* way Roger can persuade him to change his mind?

ISBN 0 09 966900 5   £2.99

KING OF THE VAGABONDS

'You're very young,' Sammy's mother said, 'so heed my advice. Don't go into Quartermile Field.'

His mother and sister are happily domesticated but Sammy, the tabby cat, feels different. They are content with their lot, never wondering what lies beyond their immediate surroundings. But Sammy is burningly curious and his life seems full of mysteries. Who is his father? Where has he gone? And what is the mystery of Quartermile Field?

ISBN 0 09 957190 0   £2.99